First World War
and Army of Occupation
War Diary
France, Belgium and Germany

32 DIVISION
Divisional Troops
Northumberland Fusiliers
17th Battalion (N.E.R. Pioneers)
20 November 1915 - 31 May 1918

WO95/2385/2

The Naval & Military Press Ltd
www.nmarchive.com
Published in association with The National Archives

Published by

The Naval & Military Press Ltd

Unit 10 Ridgewood Industrial Park,

Uckfield, East Sussex,

TN22 5QE England

Tel: +44 (0) 1825 749494

www.naval-military-press.com

www.nmarchive.com

This diary has been reprinted in facsimile from the original. Any imperfections are inevitably reproduced and the quality may fall short of modern type and cartographic standards.

© **Crown Copyright**
Images reproduced by permission of The National Archives, London, England, 2015.

Contents

Document type	Place/Title	Date From	Date To
Heading	WO95/2385 32 Division 17th Btn Northumberland Fusiliers Nov 1915-May 1918		
Heading	32nd Division Divl Troops 17th Bn North'd Fus. (Pioneers) Nov 1915 May 1918 To 52 Div Pioneers		
Heading	32nd Division 17th Northampton Fus. Vol I. Nov & Dec 15		
War Diary	South Ampton	20/11/1915	20/11/1915
War Diary	Le. Havre	21/11/1915	22/11/1915
War Diary	Pont Remy	23/11/1915	23/11/1915
War Diary	Belloy-Sur-Somme	27/11/1915	27/11/1915
War Diary	Flesselles	28/11/1915	28/11/1915
War Diary	Frechencourt	30/11/1915	30/11/1915
War Diary	Meaulte	01/12/1915	31/12/1915
Heading	32nd Divisional Pioneers (North Eastern Railway Pioneers) 17th Battalion Northumberland Fusiliers January 1916		
War Diary	Bouzincourt	01/01/1916	31/01/1916
Heading	32nd (N.E.R.) Divisional Pioneers 17th Battalion Northumberland Fusiliers February 1916		
War Diary	Bouzincourt		
War Diary	Martinsart		
War Diary	Bouzincourt	11/02/1916	11/02/1916
War Diary	Martinsart Authville	11/02/1916	11/02/1916
War Diary	Albert	11/02/1916	29/02/1916
War Diary	Albert	26/02/1916	26/02/1916
Heading	32nd Divisional (N.E.R.) Pioneers 17th Battalion Northumberland Fusiliers March 1916		
War Diary	Albert	06/03/1916	07/03/1916
War Diary	Vecquemont	08/03/1916	08/03/1916
War Diary	Albert	07/03/1916	07/03/1916
War Diary	Aveluy	07/03/1916	21/03/1916
War Diary	Albert	24/03/1916	26/03/1916
Heading	32nd Divisional (N.E.R) Pioneers 17th Battalion Northumberland Fusiliers April 1916		
War Diary	Albert	01/04/1916	01/04/1916
War Diary	Aveluy	01/04/1916	01/04/1916
War Diary	Bouzincourt	04/04/1916	04/04/1916
War Diary	Contay	09/04/1916	09/04/1916
War Diary	Bouzincourt	05/04/1916	30/04/1916
Heading	32nd Divisional (N.E.R.) Pioneers 17th Battalion Northumberland Fusiliers May 1916		
War Diary	Bouzincourt	01/05/1916	31/05/1916
Heading	32nd Divisional Pioneers 1/17th. Battalion Northumberland Fusiliers (Pioneers) June 1916		
War Diary	Bouzincourt	01/06/1916	30/06/1916
Heading	Pioneers. 32nd Div. War Diary 17th Battn. The Northumberland Fusiliers. July 1916		
War Diary	Bouzincourt	01/07/1916	04/07/1916
War Diary	Contay	04/07/1916	07/07/1916
War Diary	Senlis	08/07/1916	12/07/1916

War Diary	Bouzincourt	13/07/1916	17/07/1916
War Diary	Authieule	18/07/1916	18/07/1916
War Diary	Ivergny	19/07/1916	19/07/1916
War Diary	Ecoivres	20/07/1916	20/07/1916
War Diary	Fleury	21/07/1916	25/07/1916
War Diary	Houchin	25/07/1916	25/07/1916
War Diary	Le Brebis	27/07/1916	27/07/1916
War Diary	Loos	28/07/1916	31/07/1916
Heading	Battalion Operation Orders Nos.		
Operation(al) Order(s)	Operation Order, No. 1, By Major H.C. Oxley, Commanding 17th Battalion,	23/06/1916	23/06/1916
Operation(al) Order(s)	Operation Order No/1. Appendix "A"		
Operation(al) Order(s)	Operation Order No. 2 by Major H.C. Oxley Commanding 17th Battalion Northumberland Fusiliers (NER Pioneers).	23/06/1916	23/06/1916
Operation(al) Order(s)	Operation Order No. 3 by Major H.C. Oxley	26/06/1916	26/06/1916
Operation(al) Order(s)	Operation Order No. 4 by Major H.C. Oxley	27/06/1916	27/06/1916
Operation(al) Order(s)	Operation Order No. 5 by Major H.C. Oxley Commanding	29/06/1916	29/06/1916
Operation(al) Order(s)	Battalion Operation Order No. 6 by Lieut. Col. M.L. Pears, C.M.G.	02/07/1916	02/07/1916
Miscellaneous	Officers Commanding, "A" Company.	03/07/1916	03/07/1916
Operation(al) Order(s)	Battalion Operation Order No. 7 by Lt. Col M.L. Pears, C.M.G.	16/07/1916	16/07/1916
Operation(al) Order(s)	Operation Order No 8 by Lieut Col: M.L. Pears. C.M.G	24/07/1916	24/07/1916
Miscellaneous	Headquarters, 32nd Division.	14/07/1916	14/07/1916
Miscellaneous	Headquarters, 32nd Division. N.F.C, /222	07/07/1916	07/07/1916
Miscellaneous	17th Battalion, Northumberland Fusiliers (NER Pioneers)	13/07/1916	13/07/1916
Miscellaneous	Officers Commanding, 17th Northumberland Fusiliers (NER Pioneers)	06/07/1916	06/07/1916
Miscellaneous	C.R.E. To See and return Please		
Miscellaneous	Headquarters, 32nd Division.	27/07/1916	27/07/1916
Miscellaneous	17th Battalion, Northumberland Fusiliers (NER Pioneers)	13/07/1916	13/07/1916
Heading	32nd Divisional (N.E.R.) Pioneers 17th Battalion Northumberland Fusiliers August 1916		
War Diary	Loos	01/08/1916	30/08/1916
War Diary	Le Preol	31/08/1916	31/08/1916
Heading	32nd Divisional (N.E.R) Pioneers 17th Battalion Northumberland Fusiliers September 1916		
Miscellaneous	Headquarters, 32nd Division War Diary.	02/10/1916	02/10/1916
War Diary	Le. Preol	01/09/1916	16/09/1916
War Diary	ACQ	17/09/1916	20/09/1916
War Diary	Le Preol	21/09/1916	27/09/1916
War Diary	Acheux	28/09/1916	28/09/1916
War Diary	Bethune	27/09/1916	27/09/1916
War Diary	Acheux	29/09/1916	30/09/1916
Operation(al) Order(s)	Battalion Operation Order No. 10, by Major W.D.V.C. King, Commanding 17th Bn Northumberland Fus: (NER Pioneers).	16/12/1916	16/12/1916
Operation(al) Order(s)	Battalion Operation Order No. 11, by Major W.D.V.C. King, Commanding 17th Battn: Northumberland: (NER Pioneers). British Expeditionary Force France	19/09/1916	19/09/1916

Type	Description	Start	End
Operation(al) Order(s)	Battalion Operation Order No. 12, by Major W.D.V.C. King, Commanding 17th Battn: Northumberland Fus: (NER Pioneers).	23/09/1916	23/09/1916
Operation(al) Order(s)	Battalion Operation Order No. 12 by Lieut. Colonel W.D.V.C. King., Commanding 17th Bn. Northumberland Fusiliers (NER Pioneers)	28/09/1916	28/09/1916
Heading	32nd Divisional (N.E.R.) Pioneers 17th Battalion Northumberland Fusiliers October 1916		
War Diary	Acheux	01/10/1916	31/10/1916
Heading	32 Div Troops 17th Bn. Northd Fus. Nov 1916 to August 1917 and 1916 Dec to May 1918 (then to 52nd Div as Pioneers)		
Miscellaneous	P.A. with G.H.Q. (Sir John French) War Diary Sept 1914		
War Diary	Northd. Avenue	01/11/1916	20/01/1917
War Diary	Isbergues	23/01/1917	05/04/1917
War Diary	Poperinghe	04/04/1917	30/04/1917
Miscellaneous	Operation Order by Lieut. Col. W.D.V.O. King Commanding 17th Bn. Northumberland Fusiliers (Railway Pioneers)	01/04/1917	01/04/1917
Miscellaneous	Operation Order by Lieut. Col. W.D.V.O. King Commanding 17th Bn. Northumberland Fusiliers (Railway Pioneers)	02/04/1917	02/04/1917
Miscellaneous	Operation Order by Lieut. Col. W.D.V.O. King Commanding 17th Bn. Northumberland Fusiliers (Railway Pioneers)	07/04/1917	07/04/1917
War Diary	Poperinghe	01/06/1917	30/06/1917
Miscellaneous	Officer i/c, Regular Infantry Section No. 3	02/08/1917	02/08/1917
War Diary	Poperinghe	01/07/1917	30/07/1917
War Diary	Peselhoek	01/08/1917	31/08/1917
War Diary	St Jean	01/12/1917	31/01/1918
War Diary	Belg Sht 28 NW. A 23.C.2.3	01/02/1918	28/02/1918
War Diary		10/02/1918	10/02/1918
War Diary		04/02/1918	10/02/1918
Miscellaneous	Deputy Adjutant General, G.H.Q. 3rd Echelon, Base.	01/04/1918	01/04/1918
War Diary	Belgium	01/03/1918	01/04/1918
War Diary	France	13/04/1918	31/05/1918
Heading	War Diary of 17th Bn. Northd Fusiliers (N.E. Railway Pioneers) May 1918		

WO 95/2385

38 Division

7th Btn Northumberland Fusiliers

Nov 1915 - May 1916

32ND DIVISION
DIVL TROOPS

17TH BN NORTH'D FUS.
(PIONEERS)
NOV 1915 - ~~OCT 1916~~
 MAY 1918

TO 52 DIV PIONEERS

33rd Artmann

17th McPherrsh: Fas.
Vol. I

12/7809

Nov. + Dec 15

Nov 15
/
Oct 16

Sheet No 1.

Army Form C. 2118

17th (S) Batt. Northumberland Fusiliers (NER PIONEERS)

20-XI-15 to 31-XII-15

WAR DIARY or INTELLIGENCE SUMMARY
(Erase heading not required.)

Instructions regarding War Diaries and Intelligence Summaries are contained in F. S. Regs., Part II. and the Staff Manual respectively. Title Pages will be prepared in manuscript.

Place	Date	Hour	Summary of Events and Information	Remarks and references to Appendices
SOUTHAMPTON	20-11-15		Battalion proceeded by Rail from Cotford to SOUTHAMPTON for embarkation. Embarked 6.30pm Strength (29 officers) AND 1008 Rank + File) + 98 Horses.	
LE HAVRE	21-11-15	3 am	Arrived at HAVRE. Disembarked at 7am and proceeded to Rest Camp. Arrived Att 2-30pm.	
— do —	22-11-15	2.50 pm	Parade at Rest Camp. march to station. Entrained at 5pm. Left at 6pm.	
PONT REMM	23/11/15	5 am	Arrived - Disembarked - Proceeded by march route to AILLY-LE-HAUT-CLOCHER - BILLETED	
BELLOY-SUR-SOMME	27/11/15		marched from AILLY-LE-HAUT-CLOCHER to BELLOY-SUR-SOMME - Billeted	
FLESSELLES	28/11/15		marched from BELLOY-SUR-SOMME to FLESSELLES - Billeted 28 + 29	
FRECHENCOURT	30-11-15		marched from FLESSELLES to FRECHENCOURT - 'D' Coy (6 offrs 222 NCOs + Men) detached and sent to BOUZINCOURT to be attached to 51st Highland Division - Head Quarters A - B + C Coys proceeded to FRECHENCOURT	
MEAULTE	1-12-15		A - B - C & Head quarters marched from FRECHENCOURT to MEAULTE for attachment to 18th Division	
" "	2-12-15		Battalion took over work in trenches clearing falls improving and making Dugouts. Revetting - wiring Fire Steps and draining. LIEUT SHERRIS to England injured.	
" "	3-12-15		— Ditto —	
" "	4-12-15		— Ditto —	
" "	5-12-15		— Ditto —	
" "	6-12-15		One man wounded 'A' Coy on night /6.15	
" "	7-12-15		Work as before. — Ditto —	
" "	8-12-15		'A' & C Coys marched from MEAULTE to BECORDEL to New Billets (Men wounded Sheet /sent)	
" "	9-12-15		Improving trenches clearing falls - improving and making Dugouts improving Billets. Continued on similar works until 20-12-15.	

Sheet No 2

WAR DIARY
or
INTELLIGENCE SUMMARY

(Erase heading not required.)

17th (S). Batt. Northumb. Army Fus. C. 2118
(NER-PIONEERS)

20-XI-15 to 31-XII-15

Place	Date	Hour	Summary of Events and Information	Remarks and references to Appendices
MEAULTE	21/12/15		"B" Coy proceeded from MEAULTE to BOUZINCOURT to relieve "D" Coy who took over "B" Coys Billets at BECORDEL. - "C" Coy came into MEAULTE for duty.	Gen'l
"	22/12/15		Works carried on as usual in Trenches Improving and Making dugouts.	Gen'l
"	23/12/15		- Ditto - 1 man Killed - 1 Wounded on works (D Coy)	Gen'l
"	24/12/15		Inspections + Changing Billets &c.	Gen'l
"	25/12/15		Work as usual till 27-12-15.	Gen'l
"	26/12/15		A.C.D. Coys + Head Quarters marched from MEAULTE to BOUZINCOURT to new Billets - relieved 8th (?)Batt. ROYAL SCOTS. (PIONEERS).	Gen'l
"	29/12/15		"C" Coy proceeded to MARTINSART. Took over works improving Trenches dugouts in rear area	Gen'l
"	30/12/15		- Ditto -	Gen'l
"	31/12/15		- Ditto -	Gen'l

N. Spens
Lieut Colonel
Commanding 17th (S) Batt. North'd Fusiliers
(NER-PIONEERS).

32nd Divisional Pioneers

(North Eastern Railway Pioneers)

17th BATTALION

NORTHUMBERLAND FUSILIERS

JANUARY 1 9 1 6

WAR DIARY

SHEET No. 3

17th (S) Batt NORTHUMBERLAND. FUS RS
(N.E.R. PIONEERS)

JANUARY 1916.

Place: BOUZINCOURT

Date	Hour	Summary of Events and Information	Remarks
1-1-16 to 31-1-16		A, B, & D Companies billeted in BOUZINCOURT. "C" Company billeted MARTINSART.	
"		"A" Company:- Making New Road - BOUZINCOURT to MARTINSART. Clearing Road track - Joinering - Bottoming with Chalk. METALLING and Quarrying Chalk.	Initials/Capt
"		"B" Company:- Building Dugouts AVELUY - CRUCIFIX CORNER. - Revetting and clearing trenches - Building and framing tunnel - Repairing tunnel shaft - and sinking new shaft.	Initials/Capt
"		"C" Company:- Highland Bridge Black Horse Rd. Q.30.d.55. Draining - Escavating and building new shelters (½ Company) 5 Men killed 26-1-16. 5 Men wounded 26-1-16. 2 wounded 29-1-16. Half Company MARTINSART + BOUZINCOURT ROAD. clearing road track - Joinering - Bottoming with chalk.- Metalling ROAD and Quarrying Chalk.	Initials/Capt
"		"D" Company:- CONISTON St. Clearing trench Revetting fire bays - Rebuilding Saddly MITCHEL ST. also at PENDLE HILL - WEENING ST. Cutting back Trench Tramway MARTINSART - JOHNSTONE POST. - TUNNELING. Making RAMP.- Ballasting and Laying Tramway.	Initials/Capt

A. L. Pears
Lieut Colonel.
Commanding 17th (S) Batt Northumberland Fusiliers.

32nd (N.E.R.) Divisional Pioneers

17th BATTALION

NORTHUMBERLAND FUSILIERS

FEBRUARY 1 9 1 6

Army Form C. 2118

WAR DIARY
or
INTELLIGENCE SUMMARY

(Erase heading not required.)

17th (S) Batt. North'd Fus:rs
(NER PIONEERS)

Instructions regarding War Diaries and Intelligence Summaries are contained in F.S. Regs., Part II. and the Staff Manual respectively. Title Pages will be prepared in manuscript.

Place	Date	Hour	Summary of Events and Information	Remarks and references to Appendices
BOUZINCOURT.			"A" "B" & "D" Companies Billeted from 1st to 10th February	
			A Company. Clearing Site. Forming – Bottoming & Metalling New Road. BOUZINCOURT – MARTINSART. named NORTHUMBERLAND-AVENUE.	M.
			'B' Company Erecting dug-outs. Revetting Trenches – Digging Shaft for Tunnels Roofing Covering and Metalling Trench CRUCIFIX-CORNER. Keep No.1 POST AVELUY. DEFENCES between RAILWAY and CHURCH.	M.
MARTINSART.			'C' Company. Clearing Site. Forming – Bottoming & Metalling NEW ROAD. MARTINSART – BOUZINCOURT. named NORTHUMBERLAND – AVENUE.	M.
BOUZINCOURT.			D Company. Revetting Trenches CONISTON-STREET – WENNING – PENDLE – RIVINGTON-ST. TRAMWAY – MARTINSART – JOHNSTONE POST – TUNNEL – RAMP + RAIL-LAYING	M.
"	11/2/16 10.30 A.M.		A.B. & D Companies march to ALBERT. New Billeting Area.	
MARTINSART. AUTHUILLE			'C' Company march from MARTINSART. to ALBERT. New Billeting Area. MACHINE GUN SECTION under Lieut GORDON Billeted in AUTHUILLE from 1st to 12th 124 Guns held in reserve AUTHUILLE KEEP. NORTH – AUTHUILLE MILL + McMAHONS POST.	M.
ALBERT	11 2/16 to 29/2/16		Battalion in Billets. Employed on Construction of New Bye-Pass road N. of town; Tracks leading from Northern exits of town across R. ANCRE to CRUCIFIX CORNER. Between of AVELUY. Construction of assembly Shelters for 2 18's at CRUCIFIX CORNER. Provision of firebays in CONISTON STR: in Ft. Sub sector.	M.

WAR DIARY or INTELLIGENCE SUMMARY

Army Form C.2118

17th (S) Bn. North'd Fus: (N.E.R. Pioneers)

(Erase heading not required.)

Place	Date	Hour	Summary of Events and Information	Remarks and references to Appendices
ALBERT	26/1/16		Capt. F. W.M.S. Redwood & 50 other ranks (No. 15. Platoon of D. Co) proceeded to CORBIE for work on Construction of DAOURS - CONTAY Rline. Returned Mch 1/17.	M.J.
			P.H. Compton how in for O.C. 17th North'd Fus.	

32nd Divisional (N.E.R.) Pioneers

17th BATTALION

NORTHUMBERLAND FUSILIERS

MARCH 1 9 1 6

Army Form C. 2118

WAR DIARY
or
INTELLIGENCE SUMMARY

SHEET No. 6   19th (S) Battn Northumberland Fusiliers
(NER PIONEERS)
1 – III – 16

(Erase heading not required.)

Place	Date	Hour	Summary of Events and Information	Remarks and references to Appendices
ALBERT			Capt. W.M.S. Redmond & 50 O.R. (No 15 Platoon, "D" Coy) returned from CORBIE.	JM
			"A", "B", "C" & "D" Companies billeted 1st to 6th Moh incl.	JM
			"A" Co. Repairing & constructing road ALBERT to CRUCIFIX CORNER.	JM
			"B" Co. Defences of AVELUY. 1st to 3rd. One platoon defences of AVELUY, 3 platoons BECOURT WOOD & MAYSE REDOUBT 4th to 6th	} JM
			"C" Co. Construction of assembly shelters for 2 Bns at Crucifix Corner	JM
			"D" Co. Provision of firebays in Lonsdon St F.1 Sub-sector, 1st to 3rd. Ditto & putting BRIDGE HEAD trenches in order & revetting 3rd to 6th.	} JM
VECQUEMONT	6/3/16	9.0 AM	"D" Co. March to AVELUY. New billeting area.	JM
ALBERT	7/3/16	1.30PM	"A" Co. March to VECQUEMONT. New billeting area.	JM
			"B" Co. Railway construction.	JM
			"C" Co. One platoon AVELUY defences. 3 platoons BECOURT WOOD & MAYSE REDOUBT. Construction of assembly shelters for 2 Bns at CRUCIFIX CORNER.	JM
AVELUY.	7/3/16		"D" Co. Provision of firebays in CONISTON STREET F.1 Sub-sector & putting trenches in order. BRIDGE HEAD defences.	JM
"	15/3/16		"D" Co. No 17/1125. Pte T. CHATT Killed 4 men wounded.	Scott
	16-3-16		Major P.H. COMPTON proceeded to rejoin 6th Dragoon Guards.	Scott
	16-3-16		H.C. OXLEY. Temporary 2nd in Command vice MAJOR COMPTON.	Scott
	15·3·16		Lieut R.d.R. Dathin DALLIN. 28th Res Batt joined for duty posted to "C" Coy.	Scott
	"		2nd Lt R. FLETCHER 18th N.F. joined Batt for duty attached to "B" Coy Supernumerary.	Scott

1875 Wt. W593/826 1,000,000 4/15 J.B.C. & A. A.D.S.S./Forms/C. 2118.

Army Form C. 2118

WAR DIARY
or
INTELLIGENCE SUMMARY

SHEET No. 7. 17th (S) Batt Northd Fusrs.
(N.ER PIONEERS)

(Erase heading not required.)

Instructions regarding War Diaries and Intelligence Summaries are contained in F.S. Regs., Part II. and the Staff Manual respectively. Title Pages will be prepared in manuscript.

Place	Date	Hour	Summary of Events and Information	Remarks and references to Appendices
AVELUY.	21-3-16.		"D" Coy 2 men wounded.	
ALBERT.	24.3.16.		2nd Lt J GARVIE 32nd Batt NF. 2nd Lt J. DONALD 14th NF. and draft of 1 Cpl. and 39 men joined for duty. Posted to "D" & "C" Coys respectively	Sew/f
– –	– –		Capt A MACKENZIE rejoined Batt from Hospital took over Ct of "B" Coy 25.3.16.	Sew/f
– –	26.3.16.		2nd Lt N HOPE 28th Res Batt NF. joined Batt for duty posted to "D" Coy	Sew/f

N. Pears Lieut Colonel
Commanding 17th (S) Batt Northumberland Fusrs
(N.ER PIONEERS).

32nd Divisional (N.E.R) Pioneers

17th BATTALION

NORTHUMBERLAND FUSILIERS

APRIL 1 9 1 6

WAR DIARY

Army Form C. 2118

XXXII V(¹)

Instructions regarding War Diaries and Intelligence Summaries are contained in F.S. Regs., Part II. and the Staff Manual respectively. Title Pages will be prepared in manuscript.

SHEET No. 8 INTELLIGENCE SUMMARY 17th (S) Batt. Northumberland Fusiliers
(N.E.R. PIONEERS)
(Erase heading not required.)

Place	Date	Hour	Summary of Events and Information	Remarks and references to Appendices
ALBERT	1-4-16		"A" Coy. Railway construction VECQUEMONT.	Earl
—	—	—	"B" Coy. AVELUY. defences. 1 Platoon - 3 platoon BECOURT WOOD + MAXSE. REDOUBT.	Earl
—	—	—	"C" Coy. Construction of assembly shelters for 2 Batt. at CRUCIFIX CORNER.	Earl
AVELUY.	—	—	"D" Coy. Provision of finetap CONISTON. STREET & F, Sub Sector.	Earl
BOUZINCOURT	4-4-16	11.am	"B" Coy & with Headquarters move to new billeting area at BOUZINCOURT.	Earl
—	"	"	"D" Coy	
CONTAY	9-4-16		"A" Coy. move from VECQUEMONT - to CONTAY. Railway construction	Earl
BOUZINCOURT	5-4-16		"B" Co. Construction of roads. BOUZINCOURT - MARTINSART (NORTHUMBERLAND AVENUE) Bryc pass road	N.y.
—	—	—	North of ALBERT. Repairing to BRIDGE HEAD DEFENCES.	N.y.
—	6-4-16		D.Co. Sight-day Company training.	Earl
—	10-4-16		D.Co. Sight-day Company training.	Earl
—	11-4-16		2nd Lieut J.A. Jellicoe, 18th North Fus joined for duty 11-4-16. Posted to "B" Coy.	Earl
—	17-4-16		Capt. S.C. Walls 28th Batt North Fus also joined for duty 17-4-16. posted to "B" Coy.	Earl
—	23.4.16		St. Georges Day. Battalion had key holiday - Battalion sports were held, greetings received from Sir A. Rayestherworth - Lt Col Scott Last Director of Munitions and other Battns Nth'd Fus.	Earl
—	26.4.16		Lewis Gun Detachments fully trained and posted to Coys together with reserve sections + Guns.	Earl
—	30-4-16		"A" Company Rejoined Headquarters at BOUZINCOURT. from CONTAY.	Earl
—	—	—	"B" Company march to MEAULTE for employment on Railway construction.	Early
—	—	—	"D" Company: after completion of training employed with "B" Coy on NORTHUMBERLAND AV.	Earl
—	—	—	No casualties in action during April 1916.	

K.I. Pears. Lieut Col.
Commanding 17th North Fus. (PIONEERS)

32nd Divisional (N.E.R.) Pioneers

17th BATTALION

NORTHUMBERLAND FUSILIERS

M A Y 1 9 1 6

Army Form C. 2118

17th Northumberland Fus[iliers]

WAR DIARY ~~XXIV~~ Volume 6

SHEET No 9 INTELLIGENCE SUMMARY

(Erase heading not required.)

Place	Date	Hour	Summary of Events and Information	Remarks and references to Appendices
BOLLINCOURT	1-5-16		"A" Coy commenced 8 days training	
"	-	-	"B" Coy Railway construction Billets at MEAULTE	
"	-	-	"C" Coy Construction of ant assembly shelters for 2 Batt at CRUCIFIX CORNER	
"	-	-	"D" Coy Widening & draining NORTHUMBERLAND AVENUE also Initialing & Rolling	
"	7-5-16		10.30 Sgts to Jerusalem - 379 Sgt J Tazy Wounded when attached to Dorset Rgt for tour of duty in front section also 158. Sgt J Spensley Missing	
"	9-5-16		"C" Company marched to new Billeting area BILLon GALEEES	
"	10.5.16		"A" Company. Completed training and reserve work with "D" Coy NORTHUMBERLAND AV	
"	13.v.16		"B" Coy marched from MEAULTE to new Billeting Area. MORLANCOURT - Railway construction	
"	15.v.16		Trenches & Dugouts & Ewer Post into line Reserve CRUCIFIX CORNER	
"	"		and BLACK HORSE DUGOUTS - AUTHUILLE (4 GUNS each)	
"	"		"A" Company: Commenced night training and trenching. NIGHT WIRING completed No 1072.	
"	"		Pte J. BROWN - Killed - WOOD POST	
"	16.v.16		"A" Company continue night wiring and trenching BURY AVENUE - MONTEAGLE STREET	
"	17.v.16		"A" Company continue work on trench & night wiring 2 men wounded	
"	12.5.16		Reinforcements 1 Sgt 19 men arrived	
"	16.5.16		2nd Lt. Davey 25th NF & 3rd Lt Brennan 25th NF joined for duty. 16.5.16	
"	17.5.16		Lt Col Mc Rae admitted to Hospital. Major Daly commands the Batt. Capt King takes over duties of Second in Command	
"	16.5.16		2nd Lt. S. Bruck Battalion to Trenches 32nd Division	

Army Form C. 2118

WAR DIARY
or
INTELLIGENCE SUMMARY
17th NORTHUMBERLAND FUSILIERS

(Erase heading not required.)

SHEET No. 10.

Place	Date	Hour	Summary of Events and Information	Remarks and references to Appendices
BOUZINCOURT	F 30/4		Lt MARPLE proceeds to Headquarters Royal Flying Corps for interview	JWM
	31-4-6		"A" Company. Evening lecture at CRUCIFIX CORNER. - CONEY STREET. Sapping rustined BLACKPOOL-STREET. - Wiring BURY AVENUE - AINTREE-STREET and ROCK STREET. - Cutting tracks and removing wire AUTHUILLE-WOOD Night Work	JWM
			"B" Company. Railway Construction DERNANCOURT to BRAY.	JWM
			"C" Company. WIRING - TOBERMORY. ST. from CAMPBELL AVENUE to THIEPVAL AVENUE. Deepening and knowing trench CAMPBELL-AVENUE night work.	JWM
			"D" Company. NORTHUMBERLAND-AVENUE new road construction BOUZINCOURT to MARTINSART. Evening lecture AVELUY - Dug outs & Tramway Sidings in BLIGHTY VALLEY - AUTHUILLE Dump and tramway siding Above works are in progress and is being carried out day & night	JWM

J W May Major.
Commanding 17th NORTHUMBERLAND FUSILIERS.
(NER. PIONEERS.)

32nd Divisional Pioneers

1/17th BATTALION

NORTHUMBERLAND FUSILIERS

(Pioneers)

JUNE 1916::

Army Form C. 2118

WAR DIARY or INTELLIGENCE SUMMARY

XXXII / 17th (S). Batt NORTHUMBERLAND FUSRS (NER PIONEERS) VOL I

SHEET No. 11

(Erase heading not required.)

Place	Date	Hour	Summary of Events and Information	Remarks and references to Appendices
BOUZINCOURT	1/6/16		"A" Company. Erecting Latrines at CRUCIFIX CORNER - CONEY STREET. - Sapping near French BLACKPOOL STREET - Wiring BURY AVENUE - AINTREE STREET and ROCK STREET. cutting ricks and removing thru AUTHUILLE WOOD.	LarW FarW
			"B" Company: Railway Construction MORLANCOURT to BRAY.	LarW
			"C" Company: WIRING - TOBERMORY STREET. from CAMPBELL AVENUE, to THIEPVAL AVENUE. Improving and Renewing trench CAMPBELL AVENUE - DAY & NIGHT WORK	LarW
			"D" Company NORTHUMBERLAND AVENUE new road construction BOUZINCOURT to MARTINSART. Erecting screen AVELUY - Dugouts & Tramway Sidings in BLIGHTYVALLEY - AUTHUILLE Dump and Ramway siding	FarW FarW
			LEWIS GUN SECTIONS. Relieved by Reserve Detachments on 1st JUNE	FarW
	1/6/16		Lt MARPLE return to unit for duty.	FarW
	3/6/16		2 N.C.Os. proceed to assist LIEUT LAKEMAN + LIEUT YOUNG in the line superintending work.	FarW
	3/6/16		"A" Coy: Proceeds to Burnea Area. Received AVELUY CHATEAU carrying on same works as above.	LarW
			Lieut Col McL Pearo appointed C.M.G. His Majesty Building Honours. No 648 LpL Jaceman "C" Company Granted meladaly Granted	FarW FarW FarW
	9/6/16		Lewis Gun Detachments relieved in the line. Lt GORDON relieved Lt SADLER 8/6. Lieut RIDDEL admitted to Hospital	FarW
	9/6/16		Draft of 50 arrived and posted to Companies	LarW
	14/6/16		Daylight Saving Time introduced at midnight 11pm becomes 12 midnight	FarW
	17/6/16		Lt R.J. Marple proceeds to HQ Royal Flying Corps as probation as observer.	FarW
	18/6/16		Lt Col M.L Pearo and Capt G.D. Martin mentioned in Sir Douglas Haigs Dispatches 16.VI.16	FarW

Army Form C. 2118

WAR DIARY or INTELLIGENCE SUMMARY

17th (S) Batt. NORTHUMBERLAND FUSILIERS
(N.E.R. PIONEERS)

SHEET. 12.

(Erase heading not required.)

Place	Date	Hour	Summary of Events and Information	Remarks and references to Appendices
BOUZINCOURT	20/7/16		Draft Reinforcements. 15 NCOs + men joined from Base Depot and 2nd Lt O. SMURTHWAITE. the latter posted to "C" Coy.	Cas.H
"	22/7/16		2nd Lt. J. DONALD returned to duty with Batt. from Division Forestery.	Cas.H
"	24/7/16		2nd Lt. J. de Bosen Bindley joined Batt. for duty. Posted to "B" Coy.	Cas.H
"	27/7/16		All NCOs acting in their ranks confirmed as permanent ranks. See B0177	Cas.H
"	28/7/16		Lt Col. Paris Mt C. M. G Silenced If Strength of Batt. 26 7/6 Medical Board No. A.S. 4 a	Cas.H
"	30/7/16		Lt Col. M¹ Paris C.M.G. returned and assumed Command of Battalion	Cas.H
"	30/7/16		Reinforcements. 1 Sergt. 2 Corporals and 62 men joined Batt. from Base	Cas.H

N.L. Paris
Lieut Colonel
Commanding 17th Northumberland Fusiliers
(N.E.R PIONEERS)

Pioneers.
32nd Div.

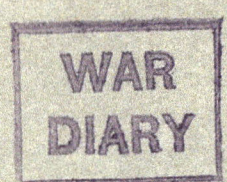

17th BATTN. THE NORTHUMBERLAND FUSILIERS.

J U L Y

1 9 1 6

Attached:

Battalion Operation
Orders Nos. 1 to 8.

WAR DIARY or INTELLIGENCE SUMMARY

Army Form C. 2118

17th (S) Batt NORTHUMBERLAND FUSRS. (N.ER. PIONEERS)

SHEET N° 13   JULY 1916

Place	Date	Hour	Summary of Events and Information	Remarks and references to Appendices
BOUZINCOURT	1/VII/16	3-30 AM	"A" Company marched off to point of assembly previous to attack	G.S.W.
"	"	4-0	"C" Company marched off to point of assembly previous to attack.	G.S.W.
"	"	4-30	"B" Company marched off to point of assembly previous to attack.	G.S.W.
"	"	5-0	"D" Company. Clear of Bouzincourt for point of assembly previous to Infy attack	G.S.W.
"			Head Quarters remain in BOUZINCOURT. Batt. in Divisional Reserve with definite orders of work to be commenced when Infantry attack has gone forward in opening up Saps. Cutting roads and Relying Trenches Artillery & transport tracks - carrying stores to forward dumps - also consolidation of Strong Points previously pointed out. Three men wounded 1-5 pm. 1-VII-16.	G.S.W.
"	2/VII/16		Companies continue work in relief day and night	G.S.W.
"			Continuation of work by reliefs day and night 2nd Lt Mucklow wounded	G.S.W.
"	3/VII/16	10/25 pm	4 O.R. KILLED 28 O.R. WOUNDED. Orders received that Batt. be relieved by 6th S.W.B. (P.) 25th Division at 6 am 3-VII-16. Coys of "B" Coy ordered to remain at AVELUY. and be attached to 75th Division	G.S.W.
"	3/VII/16		Seven O.R. wounded	G.S.W.
"	4/VII/16	8 am	"A" "C" & "D" Coys arrived BOUZINCOURT all in at 8 AM	G.S.W.
"	"	1 pm	"A" "C" & HQ marched from BOUZINCOURT to CONTAY. "D" Coy marched to SENLIS to attached to 10th Corps.	G.S.W.
"	"	5 pm	NINE O.R. wounded	G.S.W.
			Arrived CONTAY. 4-30 pm	G.S.W.

WAR DIARY
or
INTELLIGENCE SUMMARY

Army Form C. 2118

17th (S) Batt. NORTHD FUSILIERS.
(NER. PIONEERS).

SHEET No 14.

Place	Date	Hour	Summary of Events and Information	Remarks and references to Appendices
CONTAY	4/VII/16	5 pm	"A" "C" & H.Q Coys Billeted. "B" Coy Casualties 1 Killed 16 wounded. O. Rank.	Initial
—	5/VII/16	3 pm	"A" Company marched out to AVELUY for attachment to 12th Division	Initial
—	6/VII/16	—	"C" Coy & H.Q. Coy at CONTAY. "B" Coy 3.O.R Wounded.	Initial
—	7/VII/16	7.30pm	"B" Company from AVELUY to BOUZINCOURT.	Initial
—	—	5 pm	"C" Coy and H.Q. Coy marched from CONTAY to SENLIS. Lieut Riddle and 3.O.R. wounded. "D" Coy. marched from SENLIS to CRUCIFIX CORNER att.d X.th CORPS.	Initial
SENLIS	8/VII/16	7 pm	"B" Company marched from BOUZINCOURT to SENLIS. 3.O.R wounded (I.A.2.B)	Initial
—	9/VII/16	1 pm	"B" & "C" Companies marched from SENLIS to relieve NHANTS. PIONEERS on wood. OVILLIERS. ROAD - RIVINGTON. TUNNELL. Transport to MARTINSART. WOOD. "A" Company rejoined from attachment to 12th Division remained at CRUCIFIX CORNER. for work on communication. "D" Company still attached to X.th Corps for duty Casualties. 1 Killed and 3 Wounded.	Initial
—	—	—	Head Quarters remain at SENLIS. Lt. Col. Pears. acting C.R.E. 32nd Division Major Ocky 2nd in Command with Advanced Headquarters CRUCIFIX CORNER.	Initial
—	—	—	Companies located as above. (9.VII.16). works preparing Capt Wells and Lt. Donald to Hospital Sick.	Initial
—	10/VII/16	—		Initial
—	11/VII/16	—	Companies at work. SUNKEN ROAD - RIVINGTON TUNNEL - No 5 SAP and Enemy (dead) missing 24/ L/c BELL wounded. 2/Lt GERMAINE reported	Initial
—	12/VII/16	10 am	Headquarters marched from SENLIS to BOUZINCOURT. "D" Coy rejoins Batt. from attachment to X.th Corps, to remain at CRUCIFIX CORNER detailed for consolidation with R.E. Section	Initial

WAR DIARY or INTELLIGENCE SUMMARY

Army Form C. 2118

17th (S) Batt. NORTHUMBERLAND FUSILIERS (NER-PIONEERS)

SHEET No 15 JULY 1916

Place	Date	Hour	Summary of Events and Information	Remarks and references to Appendices
BOUZINCOURT	13/7/16		Headquarters Camped on MILENCOURT-ROAD SOUTH of BOUZINCOURT - Companies at work on No 5 S.A.R. RIVINGTON-TUNNEL - SUNKEN ROAD - all work delayed by heavy shell and M.G. Fire - 1036 Pte WILSON wounded.	G.S.W.
"	14/7/16		WORK going on as yesterday. D.Coy. Tramway Track from OVILLIERS - POST to CRUCIFIX-CORNER	G.S.W.
"	15/7/16		- ditto -	G.S.W.
"	16/7/16		- ditto -	G.S.W.
"	16/7/16	8/30 pm	Battalion relieved by 5th Royal Sussex Pioneers 48th Division	G.S.W.
"	17/7/16	9.30 am	Battalion marched to new Billeting Area AUTHIEULE arrived 5 pm	G.S.W.
AUTHIEULE	18/7/16	9 am	Battalion marched to new Billeting Area. IVERGNY arrived at 1 pm	G.S.W.
IVERGNY	19/7/16	7 am	Battalion marched to new Billeting Area. ECOIVRES arrived at 10.30 am	G.S.W.
ECOIVRES	20/7/16	9.30 am	Battalion marched to new Billeting Area. FLEURY arrived at 4 pm	G.S.W.
FLEURY	21/7/16	9.30	Battalion marched to new Billeting Area. BAILLEUL-LEZ-PERNES arrived 3/30 pm	G.S.W.
"	22/7/16	-	Battalion remained in Billets. Cleaning. Inspection of Clothing & Equipment	G.S.W.
"	23/7/16	-	Battalion paraded for Church Service which was held in a Meadow where Lt Col M. L. Pearse conducted the Service and addressed the Battalion on their work during the recent operations.	G.S.W.
"	24/7/16	9 am	Battalion marched to new Billeting Area HOUCHIN arrived 3-30 pm where were accommodated in shanty camps	G.S.W.
HOUCHIN	25/7/16			G.S.W.
LE BREBIS	26/7/16	9 am	Battalion marched from HOUCHIN gain to LES-BREBIS where they were billeted in new LOOS DEFENCES from 11th HANTS (Pnrs)	G.S.W.
LOOS	27/7/16	9 am	Battalion marched to LOOS and took over LOOS DEFENCES. "A" "B" & "D" Coys at LOOS. "C" Coy.	G.S.W.
	28/7/16		Lt Col Pearse took over the duties of Commandant LOOS. "A" "B" & "D" Coys commenced work on Defence rifle schemes handed over at PETIT-SAIN	G.S.W.

Army Form C. 2118

WAR DIARY
or
INTELLIGENCE SUMMARY

17ᵗʰ (S) Batt NORTHUMBERLAND FUSRS.
(N.E.R. PIONEERS)

SHEET. N° 16

Place	Date	Hour	Summary of Events and Information	Remarks and references to Appendices
LOOS.	29/VII/16	—	G.O.C. 32ʳᵈ DIVISION visited LOOS. defences.	Ersd
— " —	30/VII/16	—	Work on LOOS. Defences continued.	Same
— " —	31/VII/16	—	— Ditto —	Ersd
			Attachments to War Diary	
			Operation Order N° 1. dated 23/08/16.	
			Operation Order N° 2 —	
			Operation Order N° 3 — 24/08/16.	
			Operation Order N° 4 — 27/08/16.	
			Operation Order N° 5 — 29/08/16.	
			Operation Order N° 6 — 2/11/16.	
			Operation Order N° 7 — 16/11/16.	
			Operation Order N° 8 — 24/11/16.	

A.L. Sears Lieut Colonel
Commanding 17ᵗʰ(S) Batt Nᵗʰᵈ Fusrs
(N.E.R. PIONEERS)

BATTALION OPERATION ORDERS NOS.

1
2
3
4
5
6
7
8

War Diary   Copy No. ...

Operation Order, No. 1, by Major H. C. Oxley,

Commanding 17th Battalion, Northumberland Fus: (NER Pioneers)

June 23rd/1916.

REFERENCE MAP SHEET 57D. S.E. 1/20,000.

(1) Reference to Divisional Orders, which have been read and explained to Officers Commanding Companies, the following extracts are published for information. :-

Intention

(2) The General Officer Commanding intends to attack the enemy.

Objectives

(3) The objectives allotted are :-

(a) German Front system between R.32.c.00 and R.25.b.2.6.
(b) German intermediate system at MOUQUET SWITCH, between R.33.b.o.3 and R.20.c.8.2.
(c) German 2nd line system between R.34.A.o.9 and R.21.c.1.7

Right and Left flanks

(4) The 8th and 36th Divisions are attacking on our right and left respectively.

Artillery

(5) The attack will commence with a steady bombardment by all available guns day and night for four days up to the moment of infantry assault on 5th day (Z day).

Preliminary Moves.

(6) On the night S/T the 96th and 97th Infantry Brigades will move in accordance with orders issued.

(b) On night T/U the 14th Infantry Brigade will be relieved in line by 96th and 97th Infantry Brigades (each less two Battalions). On this relief being completed the Divisional front will be divided into two Brigade Sectors, corresponding to the present Battalion sub-sectors, AUTHUILLE SHELTERS, North and South, being allotted to 96th Infantry Brigade.

(c) On the night X/Y the 14th Infantry Brigade will move to AVELUY WOOD and the two remaining Battalions of each of 96th and 97th Infantry Brigade, and the 17th Northumberland Fusiliers (Pioneers) will move to the trenches in vicinity of BOUZINCOURT.

(d) On night Y/Z the troops will move into their forming up places in accordance with the programme. The 14th Inf. Brigade will detail troops to occupy the front system between MERSEY STREET (exclusive) and CHEQUERBENT STREET (inclusive).

Infantry Tasks.

(7) Objectives, 97th Infantry Brigade :-

(i) German front system X.1.a.6.8. to R.31.a.50.45.
(ii) The line R.31.d.8.1., R.32.c.3.7., R.26.c.3.1.
(iii) The line R.33.a.7.5., R.27.c.25.75.,
(iv) FERME DU MORQUET and trenches encircling it and MOUQUET SWITCH to R.27.c.25.75.

Objectives, 96th Infantry Brigade :-

(i) German front system from left of 97th Inf. Brigade to R.25.b.23.63.
(ii) The line R.26.c.3.1. THIEPVAL and the Cemetry to R.26.a.o.9.
(iii) MOUQUET SWITCH from left of 97th Infantry Brigade to R.20.c.85.15.

Operation Order No. 1/continued.

(2)

Infantry Tasks. (contd)

97th Infantry Brigade will detail troops to work to the right down the German front system between X.1.a.6.8 and R.32.c.o.o. and also beyond between the right assaulting column and right boundary of Division, getting in touch with troops of 8th Division on their right.

The 14th Infantry Brigade will follow the 97th Infantry Brigade moving up the valley leading from the NAB towards FERME DU MORQUET, and will attack the third objective.

The 14th, 96th and 97th Infantry Brigades will detail units to consolidate Strong Points for all-round defence.

(8) One Section of each of the 218th and 219th Field Cos., Royal Engineers will be attached to 96th and 97th Infantry Brigades respectively, to assist in preliminary work of consolidation. One Section of 206th Field Co., Royal Engineers will be attached to 14th Infantry Brigade.

(9) The 49th Division in Corps Reserve will occupy a position of assembly in AVELUY WOOD on the night Y/Z. As soon as 14th Infantry Brigade begins to move from its forming up positions, 49th Division are being moved across the River ANCRE and our present front line.

Time of Assault.

(10) The exact time for the assault will be fixed by higher authority. Zero will be the moment at which the Artillery lifts off the enemy's front line trenches.

At Zero the leading infantry must be as near the enemy's front line as our barrage permits - about 100 yards.

Engineers and Pioneers.

(11) From the commencement of the bombardment to Y day the Field Companies, Royal Engineers, less any sections required in the forward area will be collected at BOUZINCOURT.

(b) On the early morning of Z day, after the infantry moves are completed, but before Zero the Field Companies R.E. less Sections attached to Infantry Brigades, and the PIONEER Battalion will move to positions of assembly East and West of the River ANCRE selected by the C.R.E. and will be in Divisional Reserve. Tool carts ready loaded will be pushed forward when required. There first move will probably be to W.16.b.

The tasks to be undertaken by the personnel at the disposal of the C.R.E., will be :-

(i) The completion of Artillery tracks 1 to 4 (see diagram Appendix D) over our own front line system.
(ii) The completion of infantry routes over our front line system.
(iii) The opening up and completion to the German front line of at least two of the Russian Saps now under construction by 179th Co. Royal Engineers.
(iv) The reconnaissance for and construction of two routes for wheeled traffic, one in the valley from the NAB to the FERME DU MORQUET and one South of THIEPVAL to join the THIEPVAL - FERME DU MORQUET ROAD.

Dress

(12) Packs and great coats will not be taken to the forming up positions on the night preceding the assault. On Y day all packs and greatcoats will be stored : 17th North'd Fus: at BOUZINCOURT. One man will be left in charge.

Operation Order No. 1/continued

(3)

(13) Each man will carry :-

    Rifle and equipment, (less pack).
    Waterbottles, filled.
    Equipment ammunition (120 rounds).
    Waterproof sheet.
    2 sandbags in belt.
    Unexpended portion of day's ration.
    One Iron emergency ration.
    One 1-lb tin of meat and biscuits.

(b) Each Officer, N.C.O., and man will carry two fuzed Mills grenades in his pocket. These grenades are not for use of the carrier, they are intended as a means of getting forward large numbers of grenades to replenish the bombers' stocks.

(c) Wire cutters and breakers will be carried.

Transport (14) On Z day all Echelon "A" of 1st Line Transport - Limbered G.S. wagons for machine gun, S.A.A. Limbers, Maltese Cart (Medical) - Pack animals, and Officers' Mess Carts will be brigaded under a selected officer of each Brigade and will be prepared to move forward to the space SOUTH of PIONEER ROAD between W.16.a.8.6 and W.16.b.5.6. The authorised establishment of baggage and stores including Officers' Kits (35-lbs) will be packed in baggage wagons on X day.

See SQ 49/96.

Medical (15) The Medical arrangements prior to Y day will remain as at present.

(b) On Z day all wounded will be directed to the main dressing Station at BOUZINCOURT at W.7.c.3. Every opportunity should be taken to utilize empty returning transport for slight walking cases.

Stragglers (16) Officers and N.C.Os will prevent stragglers.

Papers and Orders. (17) All papers and orders are to be destroyed before the advance. No papers will be carried by Officers and men taking part in the attack except the 1/20,000 Trench Maps shewing German trenches, the 1/40,000 Map, Sheets 57D. 57C and the Lens Sheet of 1/100,00 series.

All messages and reports will refer to one or other of these maps.

Miscellaneous (18) N.C.Os and men will not fall out to bring back wounded.

(19) Officers, N.C.Os and men are forbidden to collect souvenirs.

Veterinary (20) Veterinary collecting station will be established at W.13.a.2.8.

Supplies (21) The normal system of supplies will be adhered to as long as possible except that 32nd Divisional Dumps are at CRUCIFIX CORNER and AUTHUILLE. At the commencement of operations the supply refilling points will be between VARDENCOURT and WARLOY.

Transport (22) All 1st Line Transport will be accommodated in BOUZINCOURT area as troops move East of this Village. In the event of orders being issued for the evacuation of this village on account of shelling etc. emergency lines will be as follows :

OPERATION Order No. 1/continued

(4)

Transport)contd(V.11.c.7.2 "14th Infantry Brigade, with Pioneers - to 'A' Emergency Lines, ~~V.15.d.7.4~~. On the afternoon of the 24th June the 17th Northumberland Fus: will park their wagons with the 14th Infantry Brigade at V.12.c.7.2. ('A' emergency lines, Lower Bank).

The above are marked by Boards on the ground.
When Brigades are finally concentrated 1st Line Transport is to be Brigaded under Senior Transport Officer of each Brigade.
Transport Officers to reconnoitre the ground allotted.

G.W. Martin Capt
Adjt 17th N.F.

Operation Order No.1/Continued

APPENDIX "A"

"A" COMPANY.

At disposal of Officer Commanding, 219th Field Company, Royal Engineers, vide attached programme as a guide.

"B" COMPANY.

At disposal of O.C. 219th Field Company, Royal Engineers vide attached programme as a guide.

"C" COMPANY.

One platoon will be employed in opening up end of CANDA SAP and keeping clear CANDIDA AVENUE - CANDA TRENCH to AVELUY, also opening up end of TYRONE SAP, and communication trench KILKENNY STREET.

One platoon opening up end of INVERARY SAP and communication trench CHURCH STREET.

One platoon opening up end of SAUCHIEHALL SAP and communication trench SAUCHIEHALL STREET.

One Platoon opening up end of AVENUE SAP and communication trench PICCADILLY.

Officer Commanding "C" Company will detail N.C.Os and men (as detailed) under an officer to take over each SAP from Miners in AVELUY on U night.

"D" Company.

One platoon will be detailed on U night to proceed to CRUCIFIX CORNER and repair nightly tramway AVELUY WOOD LINE and control. Keep in repair CARNATION TRACK BRIDGES.

From Y night.

One platoon repair tramway nightly AVELUY WOOD LINE, also control traffic and extend tramway to FIRST OR SECOND.

One Platoon opening up Artillery and Transport Road THIEPVAL AVENUE ROAD and JUNCTION POST LINE.

One Platoon opening up Artillery and Transport Road CARNATION TRAM and AVELUY WOOD track to X.1.7., (THIEPVAL ROAD)

One Platoon in reserve at CRUCIFIX CORNER Dugouts.

The Company, less 1 Platoon, will be located at BOUZINCOURT up to X night - U.S. Y night AVELUY Z night.

Officers Commanding A and B Companies will get into touch with Company Commanders of Divisional Royal Engineers. A copy of statement of work allotted to Royal Engineer Field Companies and Pioneer Companies is attached for reference.

War Diary

Copy No. .....

Operation Order No. 2 by Major H.C.Oxley

Commanding 17th Battalion Northumberland Fusiliers (NER Pioneers)

June 23rd/1916

Reference to Battalion Operation Order No. 1 of date. The following orders are published for information :-

1. Officers, N.C.Os and men.

The undernamed Officers will form a reserve and remain behind when the Battalion moves forward :-

(a) Captain S.C.Wells - 2nd Lieut: A.N.Pattison, 2nd Lieut: H.G.Germain, 2nd Lieut: J.C.Drury, 2nd Lieut: O.Smurthwaite.

(b) In addition, Officers Commanding Companies will each detail 1 Sergeant or Lance-Sergeant and 5 men from their Companies to remain behind. A roll of the above will be handed in to Orderly Room by 9-0 am. to-morrow, 24th instant. The undernamed are also detailed to remain with baggage as guard :-

Sergeant Irving and Shoemakers.

These Officers, N.C.Os and men will be accommodated in huts at BOUZINCOURT, W.7.c.5.3., under arrangements with the Town Major, and will proceed there on X day.

2. Rations

Application for rations for Officers, N.C.Os and men and reinforcements will be made by the Town Major to Supply Officer, or issued by N.C.O. i/c of the Ration Dump, BOUZINCOURT.

All Officers and reinforcements proceeding to join their Unit must take with them in addition to their iron rations, one day's rations.

3. Tools

Officers Commanding Companies will arrange to pack their tool wagons and panniers by noon to-morrow, 24th instant. Panniers will only be loaded with 5 picks, and 5 G.S. R.E. shovels each, i.e. 10 picks and 10 shovels on each mule. Also 4 billhooks.

4. Explosives

Officers Commanding Companies will ensure that explosives on Company charge are loaded on Company tool wagon.

5. Signallers

Signallers will carry all signalling material on the Battalion Marching out.

6. Stretcher bearers

Stretcher bearers will accompany their respective Companies with stretchers.

7. Police

Corporal Pullan and Regimental Police will march with as a party with Regimental Headquarters.

8. Water

Officers Commanding Companies will ensure that each N.C.O. and man is cautioned that water must not be obtained from any unauthorised source. There are tanks at the following points :- LOMOND CASTLE, DUMBARTON CASTLE, WOOD POST, CAMPBELL POST, JOHNSTON POST.

(b) When troops have passed over our own line into the enemy's position water must on no account be used until certified as fit for drinking, by a Medical Officer.

9. Ammunition

Ammunition mules will be loaded by Companies and will march with the Company. Also mules with tools.

Operation Order No. 2/continued

(2)

10.	Communications	Officers Commanding Companies will endeavour to keep up communication with Battalion Headquarters. 8 Orderlies per Company will be detailed, 4 with Company and 4 with Battalion Headquarters. When sending messages 1 Orderly will be sent and a second orderly at an interval of 5 minutes, with a copy of the same message. This sytem will repeat each message and make doubly certain that same arrives at its destination. On these Orderlies arriving at Battalion Headquarters they will be retained and used for the purpose of carrying messages and orders to Company Headquarters. Company Commanders will endeavour to report the situation hourly to Battalion Headquarters, and will report any change of their own Headquarters.
11.	Casualties, Reporting of	Officers Commanding Companies will endeavour to collect from Platoon Commanders reports of Casualties. Estimated Casualty reports will be rendered from the commencement of the fighting and must be the total up to date, and NOT additional. e.g. First message sent might read :- "Estimated Casualties, "A" Co., :- 1 subaltern, 20 o.r." The second and succeeding message might read :- "Total estimated Casualties, "A" Co. 1 Captain, 2 subalterns, 25 o.r.," It is most important that it should be made quite clear that the number of estimated casualties is the total for any particular Company from the beginning of the heavy fighting up to the time of the message. Estimated Casualty returns must be rendered as often as necessary. The first one should be sent not later than 2 hours after the commencement of active operations. "Nil" returns will be rendered. Accurate casualty reports will be rendered to Battalion Headquarters by 3-0 pm. and 6-0 am. daily during operations. These Casualty reports will give numbers and names of N.C.Os and men, and names of Officers (whether killed or wounded).
12.	Arms and equipment	All arms and equipment of wounded men are to accompany them to the Field Ambulance or Casualty Clearing Station.
13.	Army Book 64.	Officers Commanding Companies will render a report to the Adjutant by 9-0 am. on Monday, 26th instant, that each N.C.O. and man in the Company under their Command is in possession of Active Service Pay Book)AB64) which should be carried on the person.
14.	Battalion Intelligence Officer.	2nd Lieut: J.R.Sadler will act as Battalion Intelligence Officer in addition to his other duties. Reports should be sent to Battalion Headquarters. Instructions may be seen in the Orderly Room.

G.W.Martin Capt
Adjt. 17th NF

Copy of Battalion Operation Orders Nos. 1 & 2 sent to following:

"A" Co.
Captain H.T.Ker.
" J.E.Kitching.
Lieut: Plumptre.
Lieut: P.B.Glendinning.
2nd Lieut: J.Sadler.

"B" Co.
Captain A.Mackenzie
Lieut: J.O.Riddell.
2nd Lieut: A.G.Mitchell.
2nd Lieut: G.F.Mucklow.
2nd Lieut: J.A.Jellicoe.
(copy sent Captain
S.C.Wells for his
information).

"E" Co.
Captain G.S.Taylor.
Lieut: R.de P.Dallin.
Lieut: H.S.Cole.
2nd Lieut: G.Donald.
J.Blair

"D" Co.
Captain W.D.V.O.King.
" H.M.Redmond.
Lieut: G.V.Douglas.
2nd Lieut. W.W.Robertson.
2nd Lieut: J.Garvie.

H.Q.Co.
Major H.C.Oxley.
Captain G.W.Martin.
Lieut: P.Smith.
Lieut: A.G.Tindill.
Lieut: A.Willatt.
Lieut: G.S.S.Gordon.

COLLECTION OF STORES.

On receipt of this order Officers Commanding Companies will at once carry out the undernoted instructions :-

1. Man-handle Company G.S. tool wagons from Transport lines to Company Tool Store and load same with Company tools. (Draw cordage from the Quartermaster).

2. All spare tools and stores, such as brooms, zinc buckets, wash basins, blankets, bivouacs, fire buckets, and portable food cupboards will be handed in to the Quartermaster's Store without delay.

3. Officers Commanding Companies will inspect billets and ascertain that all Village stores are handed in. Bunks and bed cots will be left in their respective billets. Officers Commanding Companies will render a certificate to Battalion Headquarters when the above instructions have been carried out.

4. 1 Non-commissioned officer of the Quartermaster's establishment, and three men to be detailed will take over the above stores from the Quartermaster and hand same to the Town Major as required. The stores will be grouped and labelled as defined in S.Q. 4S/2, 32nd Division, a copy of which has been handed to the Quartermaster.
   This party will rejoin the Battalion on receiving instructions from Captain Marriner.

Captain and Adjutant

17th Battalion Northumberland Fusiliers (N.E.R. Pioneers)

War Diary

Operation Order No. 3 by Major H.C.Oxley,

Commanding 17th Battalion, Northumberland Fusiliers (NER Pioneers)

June 26th/1916

---

1. **Lewis Gun Detachment** — Officers Commanding Companies will arrange for their "B" Detachments (less Sergeants) to be handed over to the Lewis Gun Officer by Noon, tomorrow, 27th instant.
They will be employed as carriers to the "A" Detachments.

2. **Ammunition Supply.** — Officers Commanding Companies will render a report to Battalion Headquarters daily at 6-0 pm. during operations showing number of rounds of ammunition expended during the previous 24 hours.

3. **Officers' Kits and packs.** — All Officers' kits and packs of N.C.Os and men will be stacked in the Quartermaster's Store by 4-0pm. to-morrow, 27th instant.

4. **Village Stores, etc.** — Sergeant Irving, and three shoemakers will be left in charge of stores which are to be handed over to the Town Major.
In addition, one shoemaker will be left in charge of packs and Officers' kits.

5. **Nominal roll** — Officers Commanding Companies will render to the Adjutant by 5-0pm. to-morrow, 27th instant, a nominal roll of N.C.Os and men marching out with their Companies.
These rolls will include men left behind for various duties, but who will rejoin their Companies later (notes being made as to employment etc.) The roll should include men of Headquarters and Company Transport.

Marching Out State — (b) Officers Commanding Companies will render marching out State to Orderly Room by 5-0pm. to-morrow, 27th instant. The same remarks will apply in the compilation of this State as set out for the Nominal Roll.

6. **Details** — The undermentioned Officers, N.C.Os and men will report to the Town Major, BOUZINCOURT at a time to be notified later, for accommodation in the huts S.W. of this village.
They will be attached to that Officer for rations :-

Captain S.C.Wells,
2nd Lt.A.N.Pattison,
2nd Lt. J.C.Drury,
2nd Lt. H.G.Germain,
2nd Lt. O.Smurthwaite,
2nd Lt. F. de B.Brisley.

17/355	Sgt	P.A.Morris,	"A" Co.	17/436	Sgt C.E.Lea	"B" Co.
17/966	Pte	W.Green,	"A" Co.	17/1092	L/c W.J.W.Nichols,	"
17/291	"	G.E.Ford,	"A" Co.	17/526	Pte D.Hutchinson,	"
17/991	"	J.Forsyth,	"A" Co.	17/1105	" W.C.Abbott	"B" Co.
17/787	"	R.W.Davison,	"A" Co.	17/264	" G.W.Blair,	"B" Co.
17/1189	"	J.Masland,	"A" Co.	17/858	" W.Scott,	"B" Co.
17/772	"	E.Blewitt,	"A" Co.	17/881	" W.Wanless,	"B" Co.
17/23	"	W.R.Duggleby	"A" Co.	17/802	" T.Gowland,	"B" Co.

17/995	Sgt	F.Graham,	"C" Co.	17/30	Sgt T.Jefferson	"D" Co.
17/199	Pte	H.Camidge,	"C" Co.	17/475	Pte T.Whittleton	"
17/234	:	A.Nelson,	"C" Co.	17/499	" G.H.Crundwell	"
17/45	"	B.W.Serginson	"	17/1198	" J.Rushton	"
17/1427	"	E.M.Syrat,	"C" Co.	17/646	" W.T.Fletcher	"
17/1238	"	H.G.Smith,	"C" Co.	17/485	" A.E.Horner	"
17/275	"	T.W.Clapham,	"C" Co.			

Operation Order No. 3/continued

(2)

7. Returns   The returns at present rendered daily by Officers
Commanding Companies (Parade State; Arms, Ammunition etc.;
and Casualty Returns) and the weekly Ball and Pistol
Ammunition, Ration Strength, Stores on Hand, and certificates
called for by various Divisional Routine Orders, will not
be required after the 27th instant, until further notice.

        Casualty Returns will be rendered vide Operation Order
No. 2 and Ammunition Return vide para 2 of these orders.

        (signed)   G. W. Martin,   Captain and Adjutant

    17th Battalion, Northumberland Fusiliers (N.E.R. Pioneers)

Operation Orders No. 3.
                                        AMENDMENT:

    Reference Operation Orders No. 3 issued to-day :

Sub-order 3 should be amended to read :

3. Officers'   All Officers' kits and packs of N.C.Os and men
   kits and   will be stacked in the Quartermaster's Store by
   packs.   9-0 a.m. Wednesday, 28th instant.

26/6/16

            (sgd) G.W.Martin, Capt & Adjt: 17th N.Fus:
                                        (Pioneers)

War Diary

Operation Order No. 4 by Major H.C. Oxley,

Commanding 17th Batt: Northumberland Fusiliers (NER Pioneers)

June 27th/1916

1. Packs	All Packs and greatcoats (also Officers' kits) will be handed in to Quartermaster's Store by 9-0 am to-morrow, Wednesday, 28th instant.
2. Grenades	2 Grenades per Officer, N.C.O. and man will be issued to "A", "B", "C" and "D" Companies and Lewis Gun Detachment, also Signallers and Headquarters Company, except Transport Drivers.
3. Sandbags	2 sandbags per man will also be issued.
4. Rations	From to-morrow, 28th instant, and during active operations, the Quartermaster will issue rations to complete units of Battalion, i.e. K.

(a) Officers, N.C.Os and men actually with the Company, as required. (A.B.C and D)

(b) Machine Gun Detachment.

(c) Signallers.

(d) Headquarters.

(e) Transport.

(f) Other details as necessary.

Every endeavour will be made to inform units where and when rations will be issued.

Company Quartermaster Sergeants should hand to the Quartermaster to-morrow by noon a statement stating how the total strength of their Companies are distributed for rations, and will notify any change from day to day.

5. Cookers	Officers Commanding Companies will arrange for kettles from Cookers to be placed on the kitchens to-morrow, after the evening meal, also for all camp kettles to be taken to the Transport lines to be loaded on wagons. This must be completed at 7-0 p.m. and the one cook per Company will be left in charge; the kettles and boiler will be filled with water. Also fuel boxes will be filled.
6. Details	Reference Operation Order No. 3- 26-6-1916. Sub-order 6. Please add :-

Captain J. E. Kitching,
17/789 Pte T.Dixon, "A" Company.

(signed) G. W. Martin, Captain and Adjutant

17th Bn Northumberland Fusiliers (N.E.R. Pioneers)

Copies to:-

1. C.O., 3. Adjutant., 5. O.C."C" Co., 7. O.C. "B" Co.
2. 2nd i/c 4. Office File. 6. O.C."A" Co., 8. O.C. "D" Co.
9. Quartermaster. 10. Transport Officer. 11. Lewis Gun Officer. 12. ---. 13 Capt. S.C.Wells.

War Diary C O

Battalion Operation Orders No. 5 by Major H.C.Oxley Commanding
17th Battn: Northumberland Fusiliers (NER Pioneers).
29/6/16.

Attention is invited to Operation Order No. 4 dated 27/6/16; Orders therein will be acted on tomorrow.

1. Officers Kits.

    Officers Kits and Mess Boxes will be handed in to Quartermaster Stores at 8-0 a.m. These will be loaded on Baggage Wagons (A.S.C.) when weighed and be sent to 32nd Divisional Train at 9-0 a.m.

2. Packs.

    Packs of N.C.Os and men will be stacked in the Quartermaster Stores by 11-0 a.m. These will be handed in by Companies commencing with "D" Company at 9-15 a.m. followed by "C" Company at 9-45 a.m. "B" Company 10-15 a.m. and "A" Company at 10-45 a.m.

3. Cookers.

    See Operation Order No. 4.
    Officers Commanding Companies will arrange for kettles in use from Cookers to be placed on Kitchens tomorrow 30th inst after the evening meal, also for all camp kettles to be taken to the Transport Lines to be loaded on Wagons. This must be completed by 7-0 p.m. and the one Cook per Company will be left in charge; the kettles and boilers will be filled with water. Fuel boxes will also be filled and fires laid ready for immediate use.

4. Prisoners of War.

    All identity discs found on prisoners are to be left in their possession. All found on the dead are to be forwarded to Divisional Headquarters.
    All SOLDBUCH (Pay Books) are to be collected and forwarded to Divisional Headquarters every night in a separate bag, to be dealt with when opportunity occurs.

(Signed) G.W.Martin Captain & Adjutant,

v 17th Battn: Northumberland Fusiliers (NER Pioneers).

SECRET.   War Diary Copy No I

Battalion Operation Order No. 6 by Lieut: Col: M.L.Pears, C.M.G.,

Commanding 17th Batt: Northumberland Fus: (NER Pioneers)

Reference SHEET 57D.S.E., 32nd Div. No. 26 & special maps.   July 2nd/1916

---

1. Information	(a) The 49th Division are taking over the left Sector of our front line as far as SAUCHIEHALL STREET. The 97th Brigade hold the heel of the LEIPZIG Salient from X.1.a.8.8. through R.31.c.5.1. to R.31.c.42.42.
	(b) The 36th Division is being relieved by the 49th Division and becomes Corps Reserve.
	(c) The 12th Division has relieved the 8th Division on our right.
	(d) 75th Infantry Brigade, 1 Field Company R.E., 2 Companies 6thS.W.B. and one Field Ambulance, 25th Division have been placed at the disposal of G.O.C., 32nd Division. 75th Infantry Brigade is assembling in South-East corner of MARTINSART WOOD. The Field Companies and Pioneers are at SENLIS.
	(5) The X Corps will resume the offensive to-morrow, in conjunction with the VIII Corps who are attacking immediately North of R.ANCRE, the high ground west of BEAUCOURT Station.
2. Intention	It is the intention of the G.O.C., to attack and capture the enemy's trenches up to and including the line X.1.a.8.8. - R.31.d.15.65 - R.31.d.70.95 - R.32.a.26(b.5) and to attack THIEPVAL from the SOUTH.
3. Objectives and Tasks	(a) The 14th Infantry Brigade will capture and hold the enemy's trenches from X.1.a.8.8. to R.31.d.15.65 (HINDENBURG trench exclusive).
	(b) The 75th Brigade attacking from between MONCRIEFF STREET and GOUROCK STREET will capture and hold the line R.31.d.15.65 (HINDENBURG trench inclusive) - R.31.3.70.95 - R.32.a.2.6 (b.5.) and the trench R.31.a.6.7 - R.25.d.4.0 - R.31.b.7.8 - R.32.a.15.85, on which line it will form a defensive flank facing North. The 75th Brigade at 5-0 am., at which hour the Artillery will lift, will attack the southern face of THIEPVAL from this defensive line.
4. Artillery	The attack will be prepared by an artillery bombardment. The artillery lifts will be in accordance with a programme which will be issued later.
5. Miscellaneous	The Signal Communications, medical arrangements, water supply, orders re police, and miscellaneous instructions, will be as arranged for the 1st July in 32nd Divisional Operation Orders No. 24, which have previously been republished.
6. Distribution of Companies and tasks.	"A" COMPANY. As soon as possible after the infantry assault "A" Company will construct a communication trench from the Southern face of the LIEPZIG Salient - about point X1.a.5.9 to the head of CHOWBENT STREET. This trench will be so designed as to allow for its conversion into a fire trench at the earliest opportunity. (NOTE:) The last para of Signal Message QI/30 dated 2nd instant to Officer Commanding "A" Company is hereby cancelled.

Copy No 1

Operation Order No. 6/continued.

- (2) -

6. Distribution of Companies and tasks.)contd("C" COMPANY. As soon as possible after the infantry assault "C" Company will maintain SANDA SAP in passable condition and construct communication trench South of and approximately parallel to the same from a point near the junction of KERRARA STREET and GOSSET STREET to the original German Front Line.
(NOTE:) The last paragraph of Signal message QI/31 of 2nd Instant to Officer Commanding "C" Company is hereby cancelled.

"B" & "D" COMPANIES. Will assist Field Companies R.E., in consolidating strong points; detailed orders will be issued later.
For this purpose the Lewis Gun Detachments of "A" Company will be attached to "D" Company and any move which may thus be thus involved will be arranged by Officers Commanding Companies concerned.

7. Strong Points   The following strong points are approximately those required to consolidate the front of the objective aimed at :-

75th Brigade Front. North flank (if required).
    A 7, B 7. East Front, B 6, B 5, B 3, the East end of FORT LEMBERG.
14th Brigade Front. R.31.d.2.65. in FORT HINDENBURG, R.31.d.00., X.1.a.7.9.

8. Special Duties.   Officers' Parties which are now on special duties will so continue until relieved.

9. Messages   Messages can be handed in to the nearest Signal Office, either Brigade Headquarters BLIGHTY VALLEY, or the Advanced Station in CHOWBENT STREET.
Reports to Battalion Commander who will be at Divisional Headquarters.

ACKNOWLEDGE.

(signed) G. W. Martin, Captain and Adjutant,

17th Battalion Northumberland Fusiliers (N.E.R. Pioneers)

COPIES TO :

1 & 2 - Retained.
3. Major H.C.Oxley,
4. Officer Commanding "A" Company
5.   "   "   "B" Company
6.   "   "   "C" Company
7.   "   "   "D" Company.

War Diary

[Stamp: 17th (SERVICE) BATT. NORTHUM FUSILIERS 3 - JUL. 1916 No. 1706 (N.E.R. PIONEERS)]

not registered
before being sent out.

Officer Commanding,

   "A" Company,
   "B" Company,
   "C" Company,
   "D" Company.

     "A", "C", and "D" Companies will shortly be relieved by 6th Bn. South Wales Borderers (Pioneers).

     On relief Officers and men employed on special duties will rejoin their Companies.

     Lewis Gun Detachments of "A" Company will rejoin that Company at Battalion Headquarters.

     "B" Company is placed at the disposal of the 25th Division until further orders.

     Detailed instructions will be issued later.

     On handing over, Officers will inform relieving Officers on all points connected with the Battle tasks allotted to them, also details as to water supply, R.E. Dumps, Signal Stations, Dressing Stations etc., etc.,

                            [Signature]
                             Captain and Adjutant

17th Battalion, Northumberland Fus: (N.E.R. Pioneers)

June
July 3rd/1916

War Diary

Battalion Operation Order No. 7 by Lt. Col M.L.Pears, C.M.G,

Commanding 17th (s) Battn: Northumberland Fusiliers (N.E.R. Pioneers)

British Expeditionary Force, FRANCE. July 16th/1916

---

1. Move   The Battalion will march to new Billeting area to-morrow
"A" Co.   the 17th instant.
"B" Co.   Breakfast will be served at 7-0 am. Companies will
"C" Co.   parade at 8-15 am. and will march off in succession as per
"D" Co.   margin at 8-30 am.
"HQ" Co.

2. Dress   DRESS - LIGHT MARCHING ORDER.

3. Packs   Packs will be stacked in the Quartermaster's Stores, (No. 71 Billet) commencing at 6-0 am. with "D" Company, followed by 'C' "B" and 'A' Companies at intervals of 15 minutes.
                 This must be completed before breakfast hour (7-0 am)

                 Sergt. Shoemaker W.Irving and four shoemakers will be in charge and remain with kits until picked up by motor lorry the following day, when the party will load up and join the Battalion with kits.

4. TRANSPORT   Transport will be on the track in column of route, ready to draw out on the BOUZINCOURT - HEDAUVILLE Road in rear of the Battalion. (Pioneers - Water Duty men - and cooks will act as brakesmen when on the march).

5. Dinners   Companies will arrange that food for dinners is cut up and placed in cookers on travelling kitchens before commencing the march. Dinners will be cooked and served on the march.

6. Travelling   Kitchens will move from Billets at the same time as
    Kitchens   Companies and will form up at the Quartermaster's Store, No. 71 Billet and move off in rear of the last Company. They will join the remainder of the Transport on the BOUZINCOURT - HEDAUVILLE Road. (Transport Officer will arrange for Horses to be in BOUZINCOURT in sufficient time to move as above).

7. Billeting   Officers Commanding Companies will detail one Officer and
    Party   One N.C.O. to be ready when called for to go forward and take over billets.

8. Discipline   On arrival troops will be told off to billets and be marched into them, where they will remain until orders are given that they may leave. Necessary fatigue parties will be detailed under N.C.Os, who will keep the party in a body and march them from and to billets. No fatigue party will be dismissed until ordered by the Officer detailing same.

9. Lewis   Officers Commanding Companies will arrange for Lewis Guns
    Guns   and magazines to be loaded on Company G.S. wagons.

10. Head-dress   Caps will be worn on the march. Steel Helmets will be carried on the haversack by securing the chin-strap around the braces.

                    (signed)   G. W. Martin,   Captain and Adjutant

                17th Battalion Northumberland Fusiliers (N.E.R. Pioneers)

60   War Diary

Operation Order No. 8 by Lieut: Col: M.L.Pears, C.M.G.

Commanding 17th Battn: Northumberland Fusiliers (N.E.R. Pioneers)

British Expeditionary Force, FRANCE. July 24th/1916

Reference Map 1/40,000

1. Move		The Battalion will march to new Billeting area to-morrow 25th instant. Breakfast will be served at 7-0 am.
	"A" Co.	Officers' kits will be stacked in the Transport Lines at
	"B" Co.	8-0 am. : also any packs of men exempted by Medical
	"C" Co.	Officer, from carrying same.
	"D" Co.	Companies will parade at 8-40 am. and will march off
	"HQ" Co.	in succession by Companies, as per margin, at 9-0 am.
2. Dress		MARCHING ORDER. Caps will be worn.
3. Starting point		The head of the column will be at the Church.
4. Transport		Transport will be ready to move from Park at 9-0 am.
5. Dinners		Companies will arrange that food for dinners is cut up and placed in cookers on travelling kitchens before commencing the march. Dinners will be cooked and served on the march.
6. Billeting Party		Billeting party of one officer and one n.c.o. of 'A', 'B', 'C', 'D' and 'HQ' Company will be detached after dinners are served, and will draw cycles and proceed in advance to take over billets.
7. Officers		The following officers will proceed in advance ~~to take over, and be guided~~ and will be conveyed by bus which will arrive at the Church at 7-0 am :- (Steel helmets will be worn)

                               Commanding Officer,
                               Officers Commanding "A", "B", "C" and "D" Companies.

                               (signed)   G. W. Martin,   Captain and Adjutant

                17th Battn: Northumberland Fusiliers (N.E.R. Pioneers).

SECRET.   NFC / 218

Headquarters,

    32nd Division

       Reference 32nd Division No. S.G. 142/180 of 6th instant.   Report on Operations from 30th June to the 4th July, 1916 inclusive, herewith.

A.L. Pears

                            Lieut: Colonel

Commanding 17th Bn Northumberland Fus: (NER Pioneers)

July 14th/1916

N.F.C.
222.

Headquarters,
32nd Division.

With reference to 32nd Div: No. S.G.142/173 of 5th inst, I attach report from the officer in charge of this work.

This officer was well aware of the necessity of getting to the work as early as possible and made every effort to get his men to the site but was delayed both by hostile fire and other conditions over which he had no control.

The difficulties encountered on this first occasion will prove a valuable experience and every effort will be made in future to carry out the instructions of the G.O.C. contained in the 2nd para.

M. L. Pears Lt Col.
Comdg 17th Northd Fus: (Pioneers)

7/7/16.

17th Battalion, Northumberland Fusiliers (NER Pioneers)

REPORT ON OPERATIONS, FROM 30TH JUNE 1916 TO 4TH JULY, 1916 INCLUSIVE

Reference map : 57D.S.E. 1/20,000, and special Trench Maps.

I. In accordance with 32nd Division Operation Orders No. 24 of 18th June, 1916, the Battalion was concentrated in BOUZINCOURT on the night of 30th June, 1916.

II. Small detached parties, charged with special duties, were distributed as follows :-

    (a) One Officer and 6 men - CRUCIFIX CORNER.
    (b) One Officer and 6 men - Dugouts, AUTHUILLE NORTH.
    (c) One Officer and 1 platoon - CRUCIFIX CORNER.
    (d) One Officer and 20 men - - do -

The duties severally assigned to these parties were as follows :-

    (a) Control of traffic on Trench Tramway to WOOD POST.
    (b) - ditto - - ditto - JOHNSTONE POST.
    (c) Maintenance of Trench Tramway track to WOOD POST.
    (d) Repair of any damage occurring to banks of R.ANCRE

III. The Battalion 1st Line Transport was parked on the emergency lines S. of BOUZINCOURT - SENLIS ROAD.

1ST JULY, 1916.

IV. In accordance with para 12 (b) of the Operation Orders, No. 24, and C.R.E's instructions, on 1st July 1916, at 3-30 am. the Companies were moved to their respective first assembly positions, which were all reached within the allotted time, i.e. over 1 hour before Zero.

The Companies were thus distributed :-

1 Company in 'French trenches' and under Railway embankment to N. of BLACKHORSE ROAD.

2 Companies in 'French Trenches' and under Railway embankment to S. of BLACKHORSE ROAD.

1 Company (less one platoon) in hollow at W.10.d.8.8.

1 Platoon in Dugouts at CRUCIFIX CORNER (vide para II (c))

V. The duties allotted in the first instance were as follows :-

1 Company to open up saps to captured trenches.

1 Company, (less one platoon), the maintenance of Artillery and Transport tracks.

2 Companies, working in conjunction with the 218th and 219th Field Companies, R.E. respectively, to furnish ½ Company each as carrying parties to take forward engineer stores and to assist the Field Companies, R.E. in consolidation of captured positions; each leaving ½ Company in reserve for night work.

1 Platoon, to repair Trench Tramway Track to WOOD POST and to maintain DUMBARTON TRACK BRIDGES (vide para II (c)

Sheet (2).

1st July, 1916 (continued)

VI. The Companies received orders that as soon as the 14th Infantry Brigade moved forward, thus vacating the shelters at AUTHUILLE NORTH and SOUTH, they were to establish their Headquarters in those Shelters, 2 Companies in AUTHUILLE NORTH and 2 Companies in AUTHUILLE SOUTH. This was done ; all companies being in final assembly position within 1 hour after Zero.

The party of one Officer and 20 o.r. repairing damage to river banks (see para II (d)) having been relieved by X Corps Troops, rejoined its Company at AUTHUILLE NORTH at about 8-30 am.

VII. At this stage the following orders came into operation :-

As soon as possible after the assault

(a) the platoons affiliated to Field Companies would go forward when these did, carrying up stores to the several dumps, as previously arranged.

(b) the Company detailed to open up the saps was to push up and establish communication across NO MAN's LAND, when the assaulting Infantry had reached the first objective.

(c) the fourth Company was ordered to maintain the bridges and tracks prepared for Artillery and Transport, and when the advance allowed, to push these across our Front Trenches and as far as possible into the captured territory: also to maintain the Trench Tramway to WOOD POST and, if the opportunity arose, to carry same forward.

VIII. Owing to the advance not being carried forward these orders could not be complied with in their entirety, and the following duties were performed :-

"A" Company. This Company was affiliated to 218th Field Co. R.E. and remained in the Dugouts at AUTHUILLE NORTH awaiting the call to go forward until about 10-0pm. when two platoons were sent up by order of the G.O.C. 96th Infantry Brigade, to repair our front line trenches. Great delay in getting up occurred owing to the very heavy congestion of the C.T., which were full of wounded coming down, reliefs going up, and owing to heavy hostile barrage. On reaching the front line work was found to be impossible for the same reasons and these platoons were withdrawn.

"B" Company. This Company was affiliated to 219th Field Company, R.E. and commenced at 10-0 am., with 1 Platoon, to carry material to the forward Dumps. The material did not reach the specified dump, however, as, on the order of the Officer Commanding, 2nd K.O.Y.L.I., it was deposited earlier in THIEPVAL AVENUE. Another platoon at about the same time moved forward with material for the construction of 'hasty apron fence' in anticipation of the consolidation of captured positions. The O.C. 2nd K.O.Y.L.I ordered this material also to be dumped in THIEPVAL AVENUE, and ordered the platoon to man KINTYRE TRENCH. This platoon was later employed carrying water, ammunition, bombs etc. up to the K.O.Y.L.I. who were the old German front line trenches. It continued to carry out this duty till late in the evening. In view of the above circumstances, and on account of heavily congested trenches, as well as occasional heavy hostile shelling, the work originally allotted to these platoons made practically no progress. The remaining two platoons of this Company had been held in reserve, and at 6-55pm. were ordered forward to carry material up to WOOD POST and the LIEPZIG SALIENT. They were, however, unable to make any appreciable progress before being ordered back by Battalion Headquarters at CAMPBELL POST.

'C' Co/

Sheet (3)

1st July, 1916 (continued)

"C" Company. To this Company had been allotted the task of opening up communication across NO MAN'S LAND, by means of INVERARY and SANDA SAPS. Several attempts were made by the Officer Commanding this Company to get working parties up to these SAPS. SANDA SAP was ultimately opened at 4-30pm. and from that time onwards the work went continuously by sapping from both ends of the portion that remained to be cut to connect up with the captured German trench. As soon as a junction was effected work became almost impossible as the SAP at once became the main avenue for all troops passing in both directions.

Work in INVERARY SAP could only be commenced at 8-30pm. and was from that time on continuous until all work was suspended on the discovery being made that the enemy were still in possession of the trench opposite.

"D" Company. This Company was ordered to maintain four tracks which had been prepared for use by Artillery, and, also, in the event of the assault succeeding, to carry two of these routes forward, the one to FERME DU MOUQUET and the other to THIEPVAL.

As soon as the assaulting infantry went forward the work of reconnaissance commenced and by 9-0 am. work of repairing damage was in hand, and continued until at 2-0pm. when, owing to heavy hostile barrage, the parties were temporarily withdrawn. The work, however, was continued throughout the day and the following night during the lulls in the bombardment and the tracks maintained in a passable condition. The scattered parties of this Company suffered 16 casualties from shell fire during the day.

2ND JULY, 1916.

IX. The work of the several Companies on the above day was as follows :

"A" Company. This Company was still held in readiness to go forward with the 218th Field Company R.E. to consolidate any captured strong points. It was, however, not called upon to do so. At 4-30 pm. I ordered 2 platoons to be placed at the disposal of the G.O.C., 96th Infantry Brigade for the purpose of burying dead. These were not, however, employed.

In order to provide accomodation for other troops this Company was moved from AUTHUILLE NORTH to Dugouts at AUTHUILLE SOUTH at 8-0 pm.

"B" Company. At 12-30 am. the Officer Commanding 'B' Co. reported that the G.O.C., 97th Brigade had instructed him to make an endeavour to dig a Fire Trench parallel to SANDA SAP. Two platoons, accompanied by 2 Sections of the 219th Field Co. R.E. made the attempt but had finally to be withdrawn at 11-0 am. owing to heavy shell and machine gun fire, without making any appreciable progress. The men were then exhausted and had to be rested.

One platoon was placed at the disposal of 97th Inf. Brigade and was employed burying dead.

In the evening this Company was moved to AVELUY.

"C" Company. At 1-30 am. the Officer Commanding 'C' Co. reported that he had had to abandon further work in INVERARY SAP owing to the enemy still occupying their own Trench opposite the end of the SAP.

Owing to the relief by the 49th Division work on SANDA SAP was rendered impossible and was temporarily suspended at 3-0 am. although there were only some 8 feet or so to complete.

The congestion ultimately subsided somewhat, and through

communication/

Sheet (4)

2nd July, 1916 (continued)

communication was established by 9-50 am. A party was kept on the site to improve it and maintain the SAP and trench continuously and the remainder of the Company withdrawn at 11-45 am. to rest in view of the work that was contemplated for the following night. In the course of the evening the Company was moved from the Dugouts at AUTHUILLE NORTH to AUTHUILLE SOUTH.

"D" Company. Work on the maintenance of the Artillery tracks and Trench Tramway was proceeded with continuously. On being ordered by me, at 12-noon, to report to 14th Infantry Brigade for orders as to the provision of a burial party, one platoon was detailed at the request of the G.O.C. and worked from 3-0 pm. to 7-30 pm.

In the evening the Company was withdrawn to AVELUY, there being no accomodation available in CRUCIFIX CORNER.

X. On receipt of Divisional Operation Order No. 26, in co-operation with the C.R.E., 32nd Division, the following orders were issued :-

"A" Company would, as soon as possible after the Infantry assault on the morning of 3rd July, construct a communication trench from the southern face of the LIEPZIG SALIENT to the head of CHOWBENT STREET. This trench was to be 'traversed' so as to allow of its conversion into a fire trench at the earliest opportunity.

"C" Company was ordered to continue the maintenance of SANDA SAP and would also, as soon as possible after the infantry assault dig a communication trench south of same from a point near the junction of KERRARA and GOSSET STREETS to the original German Front line.

"B" and "D" Companies were affiliated to the 219th and 206th Field Companies R.E. respectively, for purposes of consolidating any captured strong points.

3RD JULY, 1916.

XI. On this day the several Companies carried out work as follows :-

"A" Company. The O.C. 'A' Company reconnoitred the site of the trench he was ordered to construct and considering it useless to attempt to make a start owing to the heavy shelling, and the fact that the whole length of the proposed trench was exposed to considerable Machine Gun fire from the right, he conferred with the G.O.C., 14th Infantry Brigade and Officers Commanding 218th and 219th Field Companies R.E. who all agreed that work during the day was impossible, i.e. that men would only be sacrificed and no progress made. It was therefore decided to make the attempt as soon after dark as possible. The trench was taped out soon after 10-0pm. and the whole company was at work by 10-45 pm.

At 1-0 am. on the 4th July a counter attack on the LIEPZIG SALIENT accompanied by heavy shell fire across NO MAN'S LAND interrupted the work and caused the men to take cover in the trench, ready to continue work when the usual lull should come.

1 Section of 218th F.Co. R.E. were erecting wire entanglement on the S.E. side of this trench and received the order to retire, and passing it to this Company, the whole withdrew.

The O.C. 'A' Co. estimates that another hour's work would have completed this trench as a C.T.

"B" Company. By message sent at 4-45 am. the O.C. 'B' Co. was ordered to send two platoons to assist 219th Field Co. R.E. in the consolidation of strong points. These platoons were not

employed/

Sheet (5)

/3rd July, 1916 (continued)

employed until the evening, when, at 8-45 pm. the officer i/c (Lieut. A.G.Mitchell, 17th N.F) was ordered to proceed to work in the LIEPZIG SALIENT. On reaching the German front line via SANDA SAP Lieut: Mitchell was met by Lieut: Hulton of 219th Field Co. R.E. who instructed him to relieve the working party of 'C' Company which I had ordered to dig the KERRARA C.T. This relief should not have been carried out, as these platoons were intended to relieve another platoon (of my "D" Company) working in the LEIPZIG SALIENT with the 206th Field Company, R.E. The result was that only half the intended number of men were at work after the relief. Lieut: A.G.Mitchell reports that the work was interrupted by shell fire and that at 1-0 am. the platoons were ordered to man the parapet against a counter attack. On this being repulsed work was continued until 4-0 am. 4th July. A depth of 6 feet was reached in places, but complete through communication was not established.

Throughout the night one platoon was employed collecting the dead in BLIGHTY VALLEY and burying them.

"C" Company. The O.C. 'C' Company experienced considerable difficulty in effecting a start on the constructions of KERRARA STREET Communication trench to the captured German trench. A start was made at 12-15 pm. by sapping from both ends. By 10-0pm. a distance of about 40' from our old front line and about 30' from the German old front line, to an average depth of 4'6" had been accomplished.

I consider that the relief of this Company by 2 platoons of "B" Company, carried out by order of an Officer of the 219th Field Company R.E. interfered considerably with the progress of the work.

"D" Company. 1 Platoon of this Company joined the 206th Field Co. R.E. in AUTHUILLE SOUTH dugouts to assist in consolidation work. At 3-45 pm. these were being sent forward by order of G.O.C., 14th Infantry Brigade. This platoon was employed in consolidation work and in burying dead in the LEIPZIG SALIENT. The party rejoined its Company at 12 midnight.

XII. Touch was maintained throughout from Battalion Headquarters to the most advanced parties by means of messengers, and all orders and reports reached their destination without fail.

4TH JULY, 1916.

XIII. By 6-30 am. on 4th July 1916 the relief of the Battalion by the 6th Bn. South Wales Borderers (Pioneers) had been carried out and three companies assembled in BOUZINCOURT prior to marching to CONTAY.

"B" Company was, however, ordered to remain in AVELUY and came under the orders of the 25th Division.

"D" Company was detached on reaching SENLIS and was placed at the disposal of the Xth Corps.

Lieut: Colonel

Commanding 17th Bn Northumberland Fusiliers (N.E.R. Pioneers)
13/7/1916

Officer Commanding,

17th Northumberland Fusiliers (NER Pioneers)

Herewith the report on the construction of the KERRARA Communication trench across NO MAN's LAND you instructed me to take in hand.

Q.I.31 instructing me to proceed with the work was handed to me by Major Oxley at about 8-30pm. on the night of the 2nd. just as I had completed the move of my Company from AUTHUILLE NORTH to AUTHUILLE SOUTH Dugouts. I received Battalion Operation orders No. 6 at 1-30 am. on the 3rd. By this order I was instructed to proceed with the KERRARA Communication trench " as soon as possible after the Infantry assault."

I was informed of 'Zero' time by your QI/33, i.e. 3-30am., and your message conveying this information reached me about 2-30 am. This was followed by your message QI/35 which reached me about 4-30am. instructing me to obtain details of the ARTILLERY BOMBARDMENT from the nearest Infantry Brigade. This I did, and learned for the first time that 'Zero' time had been altered. I went personally to obtain this information from AUTHUILLE NORTH, but I was prevented, owing to very heavy shell fire, in getting to AUTHUILLE NORTH and returning to AUTHUILLE SOUTH Dugouts before 9-20am. I had a party maintaining the SANDA SAP and Communication trench and from information received, and personal observation I formed the opinion that any large working party I might send up would have been wiped out without accomplishing any work. I waited for the first lull and sent up an Officer and 18 men and began sapping from both sides of NO MAN's LAND. On reaching the site of the work my party sustained one casualty and many men of the Dorset Regiment were hit, also an East Surrey Officer. However, we got to work about 12-15pm. and from this time the work was continuous. The relieving party also received casualties. I handed over the trench to the 6th South Wales Borderers (Pioneers) - Captain Evans - "C" Company, and by this time, about 5-30 am. we had got down to an average depth of 4'00.

Had it not been for the continuous Machine Gun fire across NO MAN'S LAND the earliest I could have started would have been 1½ hours earlier.

J Stamp Taylor Captain.
Comdg. 'C' Co. 17th North. Fus (Pioneers)

6/7/16

A.1.

C.F.142/208

CRE

To see and
return please.
[signature]
ADC?
27/7/16

G.S.
Noted and Returned
MCruikshank
29 July   Lt Col. BB
JWP   CRE

SECRET.

NFC/218.

Headquarters,

32nd Division

Received at 25/7/16

[Stamp: 32nd DIVISION GENERAL STAFF 27 JUL 1916] S.G.142/208

Reference 32nd Division No. S.G. 142/189 of 6th instant. Report on Operations from 30th June to the 4th July, 1916 inclusive, herewith.

M.L. Pears
Lieut: Colonel

Commanding 17th Bn Northumberland Fus: (NER Pioneers)

July 14th/1916

C.R.E. should see this & I wish to discuss various points raised by the report in view of possible future operations.

14/7/16

17th Battalion, Northumberland Fusiliers (NER Pioneers)

REPORT ON OPERATIONS, FROM 30TH JUNE 1916 TO 4TH JULY, 1916 INCLUSIVE

Reference map : 57D.S.E. 1/20,000, and special Trench Maps.

I. In accordance with 32nd Division Operation Orders No. 2 of 18th June, 1916, the Battalion was concentrated in BOUZINCOURT on the night of 30th June, 1916.

II. Small detached parties, charged with special duties, were distributed as follows :-

    (a) One Officer and 6 men -   CRUCIFIX CORNER.
    (b) One Officer and 6 men -   Dugouts, AUTHUILLE NORTH.
    (c) One Officer and 1 platoon -   CRUCIFIX CORNER.
    (d) One Officer and 20 men -   - do -

The duties severally assigned to these parties were as follows :-

    (a) Control of traffic on Trench Tramway to WOOD POST.
    (b)   - ditto -   - ditto -   JOHNSTONE POST.
    (c) Maintenance of Trench Tramway track to WOOD POST.
    (d) Repair of any damage occurring to banks of R. ANCRE

III. The Battalion 1st Line Transport was parked on the emergency lines S. of BOUZINCOURT - SENLIS ROAD.

1ST JULY, 1916.

IV. In accordance with para 12 (b) of the Operation Orders, No. 24, and C.R.E's instructions, on 1st July 1916, at 3-30 am. the Companies were moved to their respective first assembly positions, which were all reached within the allotted time, i.e. over 1 hour before Zero.

The Companies were thus distributed :-

    1 Company in 'French trenches' and under Railway embankment to N. of BLACKHORSE ROAD.

    2 Companies in 'French Trenches' and under Railway embankment to S. of BLACKHORSE ROAD.

    1 Company (less one platoon) in hollow at W.10.d.8.8.

    1 Platoon in Dugouts at CRUCIFIX CORNER (vide para II (c))

V. The duties allotted in the first instance were as follows :-

    1 Company to open up saps to captured trenches.

    1 Company, (less one platoon), the maintenance of Artillery and Transport tracks.

    2 Companies, working in conjunction with the 218th and 219th Field Companies, R.E. respectively, to furnish ½ Company each as carrying parties to take forward engineer stores and to assist the Field Companies, R.E. in consolidation of captured positions; each leaving ½ Company in reserve for night work.

    1 Platoon, to repair Trench Tramway Track to WOOD POST and to maintain DUMBARTON TRACK BRIDGES (vide para II (c)

Sheet (2).

1st July, 1916 (continued)

VI. The Companies received orders that as soon as the 14th Infantry Brigade moved forward, thus vacating the shelters at AUTHUILLE NORTH and SOUTH, they were to establish their Headquarters in those Shelters, 2 Companies in AUTHUILLE NORTH and 2 Companies in AUTHUILLE SOUTH. This was done ; all companies being in final assembly position within 1 hour after Zero.

The party of one Officer and 20 o.r. repairing damage to river banks (see para II (d)) having been relieved by X Corps Troops, rejoined its Company at AUTHUILLE NORTH at about 8-30 am.

VII. At this stage the following orders came into operation :-

As soon as possible after the assault

(a) the platoons affiliated to Field Companies would go forward when these did, carrying up stores to the several dumps, as previously arranged.

(b) the Company detailed to open up the saps was to push up and establish communication across NO MAN's LAND, when the assaulting Infantry had reached the first objective.

(c) the fourth Company was ordered to maintain the bridges and tracks prepared for Artillery and Transport, and when the advance allowed, to push these across our Front Trenches and as far as possible into the captured territory: also to maintain the Trench Tramway to WOOD POST and, if the opportunity arose, to carry same forward.

VIII. Owing to the advance not being carried forward these orders could not be complied with in their entirety, and the following duties were performed :-

"A" Company. This Company was affiliated to 218th Field Co. R.E. and remained in the Dugouts at AUTHUILLE NORTH awaiting the call to go forward until about 10-0pm. when two platoons were sent up by order of the G.O.C. 96th Infantry Brigade, to repair our front line trenches. Great delay in getting up occurred owing to the very heavy congestion of the C.T., which were full of wounded coming down, reliefs going up, and owing to heavy hostile barrage. On reaching the front line work was found to be impossible for the same reasons and these platoons were withdrawn.

"B" Company. This Company was affiliated to 219th Field Company, R.E. and commenced at 10-0 am., with 1 Platoon, to carry material to the forward Dumps. The material did not reach the specified dump, however, as, on the order of the Officer Commanding, 2nd K.O.Y.L.I., it was deposited earlier in THIEPVAL AVENUE. Another platoon at about the same time moved forward with material for the construction of 'hasty apron fence' in anticipation of the consolidation of captured positions. The O.C. 2nd K.O.Y.L.I ordered this material also to be dumped in THIEPVAL AVENUE, and ordered the platoon to man KINTYRE TRENCH. This platoon was later employed carrying water, ammunition, bombs etc. up to the K.O.Y.L.I. who were holding the old German front line trenches. It continued to carry out this duty till late in the evening. In view of the above circumstances, and on account of heavily congested trenches, as well as occasional heavy hostile shelling, the work originally allotted to these platoons made practically no progress. The remaining two platoons of this Company had been held in reserve, and at 6-55pm. were ordered forward to carry material up to WOOD POST and the LEIPZIG SALIENT. They were, however, unable to make any appreciable progress before being ordered back by Battalion Headquarters at CAMPBELL POST.

'C' Co/

Sheet (3)

1st July, 1916 (continued)

"C" Company. To this Company had been allotted the task of opening up communication across NO MAN'S LAND, by means of INVERARY and SANDA SAPS. Several attempts were made by the Officer Commanding this Company to get working parties up to these SAPS. SANDA SAP was ultimately opened at 4-30pm. and from that time onwards the work went continuously by sapping from both ends of the portion that remained to be cut to connect up with the captured German trench. As soon as a junction was effected work became almost impossible as the SAP at once became the main avenue for all troops passing in both directions.

Work in INVERARY SAP could only be commenced at 8-30pm. and was from that time on continuous until all work was suspended on the discovery being made that the enemy were still in possession of the trench opposite.

"D" Company. This Company was ordered to maintain four tracks which had been prepared for use by Artillery, and, also, in the event of the assault succeeding, to carry two of these routes forward, the one to FERME DU MOUQUET and the other to THIEPVAL.

As soon as the assaulting infantry went forward the work of reconnaissance commenced and by 9-0 am. work of repairing damage was in hand, and continued until at 2-0pm. when, owing to heavy hostile barrage, the parties were temporarily withdrawn. The work, however, was continued throughout the day and the following night during the lulls in the bombardment and the tracks maintained in a passable condition. The scattered parties of this Company suffered 16 casualties from shell fire during the day.

2ND JULY, 1916.

IX. The work of the several Companies on the above day was as follows :

"A" Company. This Company was still held in readiness to go forward with the 218th Field Company R.E. to consolidate any captured strong points. It was, however, not called upon to do so. At 4-30 pm. I ordered 2 platoons to be placed at the disposal of the G.O.C., 96th Infantry Brigade for the purpose of burying dead. These were not, however, employed.

In order to provide accomodation for other troops this Company was moved from AUTHUILLE NORTH to Dugouts at AUTHUILLE SOUTH at 8-0 pm.

"B" Company. At 12-30 am. the Officer Commanding 'B' Co. reported that the G.O.C., 97th Brigade had instructed him to make an endeavour to dig a Fire Trench parallel to SANDA SAP. Two platoons, accompanied by 2 Sections of the 219th Field Co. R.E. made the attempt but had finally to be withdrawn at 11-0 am. owing to heavy shell and machine gun fire, without making any appreciable progress. The men were then exhausted and had to be rested.

One platoon was placed at the disposal of 97th Inf. Brigade and was employed burying dead.

In the evening this Company was moved to AVELUY.

"C" Company. At 1-30 am. the Officer Commanding 'C' Co. reported that he had had to abandon further work in INVERARY SAP owing to the enemy still occupying their own Trench opposite the end of the SAP.

Owing to the relief by the 49th Division work on SANDA SAP was rendered impossible and was temporarily suspended at 3-0 am. although there were only some 8 feet or so to complete.

The congestion ultimately subsided somewhat, and through

Sheet (4)

2nd July, 1916 (continued)

communication was established by 9-50 am. A party was kept on the site to improve and maintain the SAP and trench continuously and the remainder of the Company withdrawn at 11-45 am. to rest in view of the work that was contemplated for the following night. In the course of the evening the Company was moved from the Dugouts at AUTHUILLE NORTH to AUTHUILLE SOUTH.

"D" Company. Work on the maintenance of the Artillery tracks and Trench Tramway was proceeded with continuously. On being ordered by me, at 12-noon, to report to 14th Infantry Brigade for orders as to the provision of a burial party, one platoon was detailed at the request of the G.O.C. and worked from 3-0 pm. to 7-30 pm.
In the evening the Company was withdrawn to AVELUY, there being no accomodation available in CRUCIFIX CORNER.

X. On receipt of Divisional Operation Order No. 26, in co-operation with the C.R.E., 32nd Division, the following orders were issued :-

"A" Company would, as soon as possible after the Infantry assault on the morning of 3rd July, construct a communication trench from the southern face of the LIEPZIG SALIENT to the head of CHOWBENT STREET. This trench was to be 'traversed' so as to allow of its conversion into a fire trench at the earliest opportunity.

"C" Company was ordered to continue the maintenance of SANDA SAP and would also, as soon as possible after the infantry assault dig a communication trench south of same from a point near the junction of KERRARA and GOSSET STREETS to the original German Front line.

"B" and "D" Companies were affiliated to the 219th and 206th Field Companies R.E. respectively, for purposes of consolidating any captured strong points.

3RD JULY, 1916.

XI. On this day the several Companies carried out work as follows :-

"A" Company. The O.C. 'A' Company reconnoitred the site of the trench he was ordered to construct and considering it useless to attempt to make a start owing to the heavy shelling, and the fact that the whole length of the proposed trench was exposed to considerable Machine Gun fire from the right, he conferred with the G.O.C., 14th Infantry Brigade and Officers Commanding 218th and 219th Field Companies R.E. who all agreed that work during the day was impossible, i.e. that men would only be sacrificed and no progress made. It was therefore decided to make the attempt as soon after dark as possible. The trench was taped out soon after 10-0pm. and the whole company was at work by 10-45 pm.
At 1-0 am. on the 4th July a counter attack on the LIEPZIG SALIENT accompanied by heavy shell fire across NO MAN'S LAND interrupted the work and caused the men to take cover in the trench, ready to continue work when the usual lull should come.
1 Section of 218th F.Co. R.E. were erecting wire entanglement on the S.E. side of this trench and received the order to retire, and passing it to this Company, the whole withdrew.
The O.C. 'A' Co. estimates that another hour's work would have completed this trench as a C.T.

"B" Company. By message sent at 4-45 am. the O.C. 'B' Co. was ordered to send two platoons to assist 219th Field Co. R.E. in the consolidation of strong points. These platoons were not

employed/

Sheet (5)

/3rd July, 1916 (continued)

employed until the evening, when, at 8-45 pm. the officer i/c (Lieut. A.G.Mitchell, 17th N.F) was ordered to proceed to work in the LIEPZIG SALIENT. On reaching the German front line via SANDA SAP Lieut: Mitchell was met by Lieut: Hulton of 219th Field Co. R.E. who instructed him to relieve the working party of 'C' Company which I had ordered to dig the KERRARA C.T. This relief should not have been carried out, as these platoons were intended to relieve another platoon (of my "D" Company) working in the LEIPZIG SALIENT with the 206th Field Company, R.E. The result was that only half the intended number of men were at work after the relief.
Lieut: A.G.Mitchell reports that the work was interrupted by shell fire and that at 1-0 am. the platoons were ordered to man the parapet against a counter attack. On this being repulsed work was continued until 4-0 am. 4th July. A depth of 6 feet was reached in places, but complete through communication was not established.
Throughout the night one platoon was employed collecting the dead in BLIGHTY VALLEY and burying them.

"C" Company. The O.C. 'C' Company experienced considerable difficulty in effecting a start on the constructions of KERRARA STREET Communication trench to the captured German trench. A start was made at 12-15 pm. by sapping from both ends. By 10-0pm. a distance of about 40' from our old front line and about 30' from the German old front line, to an average depth of 4'6" had been accomplished.
I consider that the relief of this Company by 2 platoons of "B" Company, carried out by order of an Officer of the 219th Field Company R.E. interfered considerably with the progress of the work.

"D" Company. 1 Platoon of this Company joined the 206th Field Co. R.E. in AUTHUILLE SOUTH dugouts to assist in consolidation work. At 3-45 pm. these were being sent forward by order of G.O.C., 14th Infantry Brigade. This platoon was employed in consolidation work and in burying dead in the LEIPZIG SALIENT. The party rejoined its Company at 12 midnight.

XII. Touch was maintained throughout from Battalion Headquarters to the most advanced parties by means of messengers, and all orders and reports reached their destination without fail.

4TH JULY, 1916.

XIII. By 6-30 am. on 4th July 1916 the relief of the Battalion by the 6th Bn. South Wales Borderers (Pioneers) had been carried out and three companies assembled in BOUZINCOURT prior to marching to CONTAY.
"B" Company was, however, ordered to remain in AVELUY and came under the orders of the 25th Division.
"D" Company was detached on reaching SENLIS and was placed at the disposal of the Xth Corps.

A.L. Pears.
Lieut: Colonel
Commanding 17th Bn Northumberland Fusiliers (N.E.R. Pioneers
13/7/1916

32nd Divisional (N.E.R) Pioneers

17th BATTALION

NORTHUMBERLAND FUSILIERS

AUGUST 1 9 1 6

WAR DIARY or INTELLIGENCE SUMMARY

Army Form C. 2118

17th (S) Batt NORTHUMBERLAND FUSRs.
(NER. PIONEERS)

SHEET No 17

Place	Date	Hour	Summary of Events and Information	Remarks and references to Appendices
LOOS	1/VIII/16		A.B.D. and Headquarters work on Defences. 'C' Coy at PETIT-SAINS and working on Dugouts for Bomb Stores. 15th Pte E. BRUCE 'A' Coy killed and Aircraft Shell.	
"	2/VIII/16		— ditto —	
"	3/VIII/16		— ditto — 1223. Pte A. Davidson slightly wounded duty	
"	4/VIII/16		ditto. Lt Col McPenro C.M.G. admitted to Hospital sick — OC 'C' Coy and 1NCO proceeded from PETIT-SAINS to ANNEQUIN to take over Billets for 'C' Coy. Armourers on S	
"	5/VIII/16	1 pm	'C' Coy moved from PETIT-SAINS to ANNEQUIN to Billets and took over work. Major H.C. Ocley took over temporary Command of Battalion Major King acting Temporary Second in Command	
"	6/VIII/16		— ditto — wrote A, B & D Coys as on 4 E. 'C' Coy took over mining + sapping at ANNEQUIN	
"	7/VIII/16		— ditto —	
"	8/VIII/16		— ditto —	
"	9/VIII/16		Advised that 2 men attached to Divisional Head Quarters were killed during bombardment of BETHUNE on 7th inst Transport moved to P.SAINS to NOEUX LE MINES	
"	10/VIII/16		'D' Coy ordered to commence repair of front line HARRISON + HART CRATER.	
"	11/VIII/16		Companies working as above	
"	14/VIII/16		No 353. Pte Richardson 'B' Coy wounded Cable Trench.	
"	16/VIII/16		Major Ocley proceeded to Headquarters Division attached for special duty. Major King assume Temporary Command of Battalion	
"	17/VIII/16		A, B, C + D Coys work in respective areas as usual.	

WAR DIARY or INTELLIGENCE SUMMARY

Army Form C. 2118

17th (S) Batt. NORTHUMBERLAND FUSILIERS
(N.E.R. PIONEERS)

SHEET No. 18

Place	Date	Hour	Summary of Events and Information	Remarks and references to Appendices
LOOS	18th		A, B, C & D Coys work as usual. CHURCH of ENGLAND Service at Headquarters.	G.S.H
"	19th		A, B & D Coys work as usual. LOOS Defences - C Coy mining ANNEQUIN road	G.S.H
"	20th		Ditto	G.S.H
"	21st		Ditto	G.S.H
"	22nd		Ditto	G.S.H
"	23rd		Ditto	G.S.H
"	24th		Ditto	G.S.H
"	25th		Ditto	G.S.H
"	26th		Ditto	G.S.H
"	26th		Ditto	G.S.H
"	29th		B Coy moved from LOOS to ANNEQUIN.	G.S.H
"	30th		A Coy moved from LOOS to ANNEQUIN. B Coy & Headquarters A LE PREOL. Lewis Guns and Detachment remained in position LOOS Defences. One man 'A' Coy wounded at ANNEQUIN	G.S.H
LE PREOL	31st		A, C & D Coys Billeted at ANNEQUIN - B Coy and Headquarters Billeted at LE PREOL. Taking over work in new Sectors. TRANSPORT LINES Billed at NOEUX-LE-MINES.	G.S.H

[signature]
Major.
Commanding 17th Northumberland Fus.
(N.E.R. PIONEERS)

32nd Divisional (N.E.R) Pioneers

17th BATTALION

NORTHUMBERLAND FUSILIERS

SEPTEMBER 1 9 1 6

Headquarters,

32nd Division

CONFIDENTIAL.

[Stamp: 17th (SERVICE) BATT. NORTH'D FUSILIERS, 2 - OCT. 1916, (N.E.R. PIONEERS)]

WAR DIARY.

Herewith please find War Diary of this Unit for month ending September 30th/1916.

Please acknowledge receipt.

[Signature] Capt.
for Lieut: Colonel
Comdg: 17th Bn Northumberland Fus
(NER Pioneers)

October 1st/1916

Vol 10.

Army Form C. 2118

WAR DIARY or INTELLIGENCE SUMMARY

17½(S) Batt. NORTHUMBERLAND. FRS. (N.E.R. PIONEERS)

SHEET No 19

(Erase heading not required.)

Place	Date	Hour	Summary of Events and Information	Remarks and references to Appendices
LE PREOL	1-9-16		A. C. D. Coys. ANNEQUIN in billets and work in sector MINING - CABLE TRENCH. B Coy & Head Quarters. LE PREOL in billets - Capt Taylor took over duties of 2nd in Cd.	Genl
"	2.9.16		Lewis Guns and Detachments relieved from LOOS defences. Regain A.C & D coys at ANNEQUIN.	Genl
"	3.9.16		Capt J.B. Bragge. 28th Batt and 2nd Lt E.W Smith 32nd Batt joined the Batt for duty 29.8.16. 2nd Lieut E.R Neville 32nd Batt joined Batt for duty 3.9.16	Genl
"	4.9.16		Listed on Cable trench and road works in line	Genl
"	5.9.16		Reinforcements 2 Corporals and 1 Lce beyond from Base	Genl
"	6.9.16		Companies A.C + D located at ANNEQUIN Bn Headquarters at LE PREOL went as usual	Genl
"			Companies went as usual until 16th Sept 1916	Genl
"	16.9.16		Battalion ordered to move to ACQ by Rcute Route on 17th	Genl
ACQ	17.9.16		Battalion marched at 8.30am arrive ACQ at 5pm	Genl
"	18.9.16		Battalion remained in billets the 12 noon marched Bn's training in trenches for work, very wet and muddy. Rainy Vile day.	Genl
"	19.9.16		Battalion visited from trenches and returned ACQ to billets	Genl
"	20.9.		Battalion marched from ACQ to LE PREOL and ANNEQUIN arrived at 5pm Took over work as before. Lt. SHUTSON & 2nd Lt N WATSON joined Bn	Genl
LE PREOL	22.9.16		Battalion ordered to move by rail at 5pm	Genl
LE PREOL	23.9.16		Orders for move cancelled.	Genl
	24.9.16.			Genl

Army Form C. 2118

WAR DIARY
or
INTELLIGENCE SUMMARY

17th (S) Batt. NORTHUMBERLAND FRS
(N.E.R. PIONEERS)

SHEET No 20.

(Erase heading not required.)

Instructions regarding War Diaries and Intelligence Summaries are contained in F.S. Regs., Part II. and the Staff Manual respectively. Title Pages will be prepared in manuscript.

Place	Date	Hour	Summary of Events and Information	Remarks and references to Appendices
LE PREOL	Sept. 26th		Battalion ordered to move to new Billeting area on 27th by rail	G.S./U
"	27th		Battalion left ANNEQUIN - LE PREOL 9 a.m. 27th marched to BETHUNE	G.S./U
			Station at 11.50 a.m. train moved off for ACHEUX arrived at 7-30 p.m.	G.S./U
			Battalion bivouack'd in WOOD for night and commenced work on	
			railway construction. "D" Coy to MARTINSART WOOD. "A" Coy to MAILLY-MAILLET	G.S./U
ACHEUX	28th		"B" and "C" Coys remained at ACHEUX WOOD. together with Headquarters	G.S./U
			Companies commenced distribution of Kit (rails + sleepers) and opening	
			up track for front gauge line from " to AVELUY.	G.S./U
BETHUNE	27th		Left advance party Battalion arrived for tracking to 19th N.F.	G.S./U
ACHEUX	29th		Reinforcements of 6 men arrived	G.S./U
"	30th		Railway construction continued.	G.S./U

W. D. Phh.
Lieut Colonel.
Commanding 17th (S) Batt. Northd Fusrs.
(N.E.R. PIONEERS)

War Diary

Battalion Operation Order No. 10, by Major W.D.V.C.King,

Commanding 17th Bn Northumberland Fus: (NER Pioneers):

British Expeditionary Force, FRANCE.

Midnight, SEPTEMBER 16th/1916

1. Move	The Battalion will move to new billeting area to-morrow the 17th. Instant by the road NOEUX-les-MINES - HERMIN - GRAND SERVINS - CAMBLAIN L'ABBE to ACQ and ECOIVRES.
2. Advance Party	Lieut: W.W.ROBERTSON, "B" Company and 8 o.r. will proceed by bus which will be met at Cross Roads, BEUVRY at 7/45 am. This party will consist of 1 o.r. of "A", "B", "C" and "D" Kitchens
3. Transport	"A","C" and "D" Companies/and one Water cart will be collected at 8/0 am. and proceed direct to the Transport Lines. One Baggage wagon (ASC) will pick up Officers' Kits and Mess Boxes of "A","C" and "D" Companies at the same hour. One Baggage wagon (ASC) will pick up "HQ" and "B" Co., Officers' Kits at 8/0 am. at LE PREOL and return to Quartermaster's Store for remainder of load.
4. Packs and blankets.	Lorries to carry packs and blankets will be provided, and will be at Company Headquarters at 8/0 am. 1 A, 1 B, 1 C 1 D Companies.
5. Maltese Cart.	Maltese Cart for Medical equipment will be sent to LE PREOL and loaded at 8/30 am.
6. Order of march.	"A","C" and "D" Companies will march from ANNEQUIN at intervals of 3 minutes between platoons: the leading platoon will leave in sufficient time so as to allow of the whole party being clear of the Cross Roads at F.27.c.7.9. at 9/30am on the LAVENTIE ROAD (Sheet 36B.NW.) "B" Company will march off at 8/45 am. as a company intact. Transport will march from BEUVRY at 9/0 am. and will halt with head at Cross roads at F.27.c.7.9. The Battalion will march from above point at 10/0 am.
7. Dress	LIGHT MARCHING ORDER - Steel helmets will be carried on the Haversack.
8. Dinners	Dinners will be cooked on the march.
9. 32nd Divnl School	Lieut: P.S.GLENDINNING, his batman and Sergeant proceeding to Divisional School on the 18th. instant, also the two pioneers who are to report at the School on the 20th instant will remain behind and be attached to Major OXLEY's party.
10. 1st Army School	Lieut: R.A.LANGHAM, his batman, and 17/393 Sgt T.D.SHARES "D" Co. will proceed to BETHUNE to-morrow, vide instructions issued.
11. Rear Party	Lieut: J.JARVIS will march rear party and pick up stragglers.
12. Billets	Officers Commanding Companies will take special steps to ensure that all billets are left clean and in a sanitary condition.
2. Pioneers	Pioneer Sergt. J.S.WATSON and artificers will proceed to Transport lines at 8/0 am and report to the Quartermaster. They will act as brakesmen on the march.

ACKNOWLEDGE RECEIPT.

(Signed) G. H. Martin, Captain and Adjutant
17th Bn Northumberland Fusiliers (N.E.R. Pioneers)

Battalion Operation Order No. 11 by Major W.D.V.O.King, War Diary.

Commanding 17th Battn: Northumberland Fus:(NER Pioneers).

British Expeditionary Force FRANCE.

19th September/16.

---

1. **Move.** The Battalion will move to new Billeting Area tomorrow the 20th inst by road CAMBLAIN-LE-ABBE - GRAND SERVINE - HERSIN - NOEUX-LES-MINES - LE PREOL - ANNEQUIN.

2. **Advance Party.** Officer Commanding "C" Company will detail an Officer to take charge of Billeting party which will consist of one N.C.O. from each Company - "A" "B" "C" "D" & "HQ".

3. **Breakfast.** Breakfast will be served at 6-30 a.m.

4. **Kits, Packs & Blankets.** Officers Kits, packs and blankets will be stacked ready for loading on Motor Lorries at 7-30 a.m. in the following order - A, B & HQ, C, and D (4 lorries).

5. **Point of Assembly.** Point of assembly will be at the "U" in PENDU on the ARRAS ROAD at 9-0 a.m. Reference Map - LENS, 11, Sheet 1/100,000.

6. **Order of March.** Companies will move off in the following order "B" "C" "D" "A" and "HQ", and will march off to starting point at 8-30 a.m.

7. **Dress.** Light Marching Order - Steel Helmets will be carried on Haversack.

8. **Lewis Guns.** Lewis Guns and Detachments will march in front of Transport.

9. **Dinners.** Dinners will be cooked on the march.

10. **Sick Men.** All sick men unable to march who are certified by the Medical Officer will go in Motor Lorries and will act as off-loading party.

11. **Course of Cookery.** Officers Commanding "C" and "D" Companies will arrange for the men who are attending Cookery Course to parade at 8-30 a.m. and march to ECOIVRES and report to the Adjutant, 2nd Dorset Regt: They will join that Unit's party and proceed by Bus under an Officer. Haversack rations for the day will be carried by the two men.

12. **Rear Party.** An Officer will be detailed to march in rear of the Battalion and form a rear party if necessary.

13. **Billets.** Officers Commanding Companies will take special steps to ensure that Billets are left clean and sanitary, and will report that they have been inspected by an Officer before marching off.

(Signed) G.W.Martin Captain & Adjutant,

17th Battn: Northumberland Fusiliers (NER Pioneers).

C.O.

Battalion Operation Order No. 12. by Major W.D.V.O.King

Commanding 17th Battn: Northumberland Fus: (NER Pioneers).

23rd September/16.

1. Move.	The Battalion will move to new Billeting area tomorrow Sunday, the 24th inst, by rail.
2. Breakfast.	Breakfast will be served at 6-0 a.m.
3. Officers Kits & Blankets.	Officers Kits and blankets will be stacked ready for loading on Motor Transport at 6-0 a.m.
4. Advanced Party.	"B" Company will parade at 7-0 a.m. so as to arrive at BETHUNE STATION at 8-0 a.m. and will assist to load Transport on Wagons and off-load blankets and Officers Kits from Motor Transport. The Officers Kits will be packed on A.S.C. Baggage wagons by "B" Company at the Station.
5. Transport.	Transport of the Battalion will arrive at BETHUNE STATION at 8-0 a.m. Wagons will be loaded and Horses and Mules boxed. The Transport Officer will arrange for feeds to be carried handy for animals, also water buckets to enable watering on the journey.
6. Machine Guns.	Officer Commanding "B" Company will detail a party of two N.C.Os and 30 men to man handle the hand-carts to the Station which will be picked up at the Transport Lines, BEUVRY.
7. Order of the March.	Officers Commanding "A" "C" "D" Companies will march off in the above order by platoons from ANNEQUIN to BEUVRY commencing with first platoon of "A" Company at 8-15 a.m. 5 minutes interval between platoons. After BEUVRY Companies will march intact at intervals of 300 yards.
8. Kitchens & Water Carts.	Kitchens and Water Carts will be collected at ANNEQUIN at 7-0 a.m. Headquarter Company's Water Cart and "B" Co's Kitchen will be collected at 7-0 a.m. and will proceed direct to Station. Water Carts will be filled at the Station.

(Signed) G.W.Martin Captain & Adjutant,

17th Battn: Northumberland Fusiliers (NER Pioneers).

War Diary

Battalion Operation Order No. 12 by Lieut. Colonel W.D.V.O.King,
Commanding 17th Bn. Northumberland Fusiliers (NER Pioneers)
British Expeditionary Force.
26th September 1916.

---

1. **MOVE.** The Battalion will move to new Billeting area to-morrow Wednesday the 27th inst. by rail.

2. **BREAKFAST.** Breakfasts will be served at 7-0 a.m.

3. **OFFICERS KITS and mens BLANKETS.** Officers kits and mens blankets will be stacked ready for loading on Motor Transport at 8-0 a.m.

4. **ADVANCE PARTY.** Officer Commanding "B" Company will detail 2 Officers and 100 NCOs and men to parade, and march off at 7-30 a.m. to assist to load Transport on wagons and off load blankets and Officers kits from Motor transport. The Officers kits will then be packed on A.S.C. Baggage wagons by "B" Company at the Station.

5. **TRANSPORT.** Transport of the Battalion will arrive at BETHUNE station at 8-30 a.m. wagons will be loaded and horses boxed at once. Horses and mules will be boxed with harness on. The Transport Officer will arrange for feeds to be carried handy for the animals, also water buckets to enable watering on the journey if necessary.

6. **MACHINE GUNS.** Officer Commanding "B" Company will detail a party of two NCOs and 36 men of the above, 100, to man handle the Lewis Gun hand-carts to the station which will be picked up at the Transport Lines BEUVRY.

7. **ORDER of MARCH.** O.C. "A" "C" & "D" Companies will march off in the above order by platoons from ANNEQUIN to BEUVRY commencing with first platoon of "A" Co. at 8-15 a.m. After BEUVRY Companies will march intact at intervals of 300 yards, so as the last Company arrives at BETHUNE station at 10-30am.
The remainder of "B" Company will march from LE PREOL at 8-30 am.

8. **WATER CARTS.** Water carts will be filled at the Railway Station and loaded full, and will each have their compliment of canvas buckets handy for distribution of water by Water Duty men if necessary.

9. **TRAVELLING KITCHENS.** Travelling kitchens will have fires laid and dinners ready for cooking in the Cookers before being loaded.

10. **REPORTS.** Officers Commanding Companies will report on arrival at BETHUNE Station the state of their Companies, and will also hand over to the Adjutant marching out States which will give the following particulars only:-
No. of Officers - Warrent Officers - Staff Sergeants - Sergeants - Lance-Sergeants - Corporals - Lance Corporals and privates marching out and entraining with the Battalion.

11. **Officers Chargers.** Officers Chargers must arrive at BETHUNE station for boxing by 9-30 am.

(Signed) G.W.Martin, Captain & Adjutant,
17th Bn. Northumberland Fusiliers (NER Pioneers)

32nd Divisional (N.E.R.) Pioneers

17th BATTALION

NORTHUMBERLAND FUSILIERS

OCTOBER 1 9 1 6

Vol 11

Army Form C. 2118

WAR DIARY
or
INTELLIGENCE SUMMARY

17th (S) Batt. NORTHUMBERLAND FUSRS.
(N.E.R-PIONEERS)

SHEET No 21

Place	Date	Hour	Summary of Events and Information	Remarks and references to Appendices
ACHEUX	1/x/16.		A Company at MAILLY-MAILLET. 'D' Coy MARTINSART WOOD. B + C Coys and Headquarters at ACHEUX WOOD Railway construction.	G.S.M
"	2/x/16.		— Do —	Esv.1.
"	6.x.16.		— Do —	G.S.M
"	7.x.16.		— Do — 2 men 'C' Coy wounded Shrapnel	G.S.M
"	9.x.16.		'C' Coy moved from ACHEUX WOOD to ENGLEBELMER to Billets.	G.S.M
"			'B' Coy moved from ACHEUX WOOD to MARTINSART to Billets. Headquarters and Transport only at ACHEUX WOOD.	G.S.M
"	15.x.16		Transport moved from ACHEUX WOOD to 'D' LINES ACHEUX	P.1.
"	20.x.16.		'A' Coy moved from MAILLY-MAILLET to P17 & 3.3 ALBERT combined Casualties Lieut PLUMTRE slightly wounded Sheet 57060 at duty. 2 slightly wounded at duty.	P.1.
			1 killed 12 wounded	P.S.
"	27/x/16.		A Company moved from P17 & 3.3. to camp site opposite PIONEER ROAD.	G.S.M
"	31/x/16.		Headquarters of Batt. moved from ACHEUX WOOD to No 2 QUARRY-NORTH D. AVENUE. Headquarters MARTINSART.	G.S.M

Wg. Lt. Colonel
Comdg 17th NF (N.E.R. PIONEERS)

32 DIV TROOPS

17th Bn: North'd Fus:

Nov: 1916 to August 1917
and
1916 DEC
~~Dec 1917~~ to May 1918.
(then to 52nd Div as Pioneers)

DEC 17 Railway Troops
LofC TRANS UNITS

Aug 18 52 DIV Troops
(PIONEERS)

Box ~~2781~~

P.A. with G.H.Q. (Sir John French) War Diary
Sept. 1914

"Contemptible little army"

Origin of phrase - vide
R.O. of 24th September 1914

WAR DIARY
or
INTELLIGENCE SUMMARY

Army Form C. 2118

17th (S) Batt. NORTHUMBERLAND FUSRS
(N.E.R. PIONEERS).

NOVEMBER 1916

SHEET No. 22.

(Erase heading not required.)

Place	Date	Hour	Summary of Events and Information	Remarks and references to Appendices
NARTH D. AVENUE.	1/11/16		A & C Coys. Camped on PIONEER ROAD, working on Railway Construction	
			B & D Coys. Camped and in Dugouts Sunken Road MARTINSART WOOD	
	1/11/16		Lt Parthimay rejoined Batt. for duty from 32nd Divisional School	
	5/11/16		Lt Blair proceeded to Royal Flying Corps on Probation on being medically unfit	
			Lt Pendenny took over Command of 'A' Coy 1/11/16 vice Capt H T Ker	
	24/11/16		Lt P. Dallin rejoined Batt. for duty from Employment, was CR.E.32nd Division	
	25/11/16		Lt Douglas to command 'D' Coy vice Capt Hitching	
			Capt Hitching proceed to E.O.R. for employment as Railway Transportation Department	
			Draft Reinforcement 24 men the Batt.	
	14/11/16		Battalion to be converted into a Railway Pioneer Batt. on the Est. Ia Labour Battalion Royal Engineers (Authy F.H.Q. A&A 1883q 9th/12th.)	
	15 &		Companies working on Railway Construction under 277th Coy R.E.	
	30			

Lt W Jardin Capt(Adjt)
for O.C. 17th NF.

12.(1)

Army Form C. 2118

WAR DIARY
or
INTELLIGENCE SUMMARY

17th (S) Batt NORTH'D FUSRS
(RAILWAY PIONEERS) DECEMBER 1916

SHEET No. 23.

Place	Date	Hour	Summary of Events and Information	Remarks and references to Appendices
NORTH'L'D AVENUE	1/12/16. 31/12/16		A. & C. Coys. Camped on PIONEER ROAD working on railway construction.	Offy
	1/12/16. 7/12/16		B. & D. Coys. Camped + in dugouts, sunken road. MARTINSART WOOD. Railway construction.	Offy
	9/12/16. 31/12/16		B. Coy. Moved to new camping area near Beaussart. Railway construction.	Offy
	7/12/16. 19/12/16		D. Coy. Moved to new camping area near Beaussart. Railway construction.	Offy
	18/12/16. 31/12/16		D. Coy. moved to new camping area near Raincheval. Railway construction.	Offy
	19/12/16		Draft reinforcement 150 or joined Battn.	Offy
	21/12/16		Draft reinforcement 75 or joined Battn	Offy
	22/12/16		Capt Martin proceeded to G.H.Q. for temporary duty with D.G.T.	Offy
	29/12/16.		Draft reinforcement 5 or joined Battn.	Offy
			Battalion engaged on railway construction under 277th Coy. R.E.	Offy

M. King
Comdg 17th NF (RAILWAY PIONEERS)
Lt-Col

WAR DIARY

Army Form C. 2118

19th Bn. Northumberland Fusiliers (Railway Pioneers)

SHEET No. 24

Place	Date	Hour	Summary of Events and Information	Remarks and references to Appendices
NORTHD. AVENUE	1.1.17		A and E Companies camped on Pioneer Road working on railway construction. B Company at BERUSSART working on Railway Construction. D Company at RAINCHEVAL working on Railway construction under C.O.R.C.C. Detachment of 2 officers, 28 O.R. at THIENNES – working on Light Railway Depot.	
	6.1.17		A Company moved to CANDAS - Railway Construction under 277 Railway Co.	
	13.1.17		17/095 Pte. J.T. Johnson B Coy Killed	
	20.1.17		"C" Company moved to HOULERON for work on Light Railway Depot. Detachment of 1 Officer 58 O.R. proceeded for temporary duty at No.1 Railway Depot. Detachment of 1 Officer 70 O.R. proceeded for temporary duty with A.D.L.R. First Army.	
ISBERGUES	23.1.17		Battalion Headquarters moved to new Billeting area ISBERGUES 23-1-1917.	
	25.1.17		B Co. moved to new Billeting area at LA LACQUE 23-1-1917. D Co. moved to new Billeting area at LA ROUPIE 25-1-1917.	
	31.1.17		HQ. B. C. & D Companies employed on construction of Light Rly. Repair Shops, BERGUETTE. A Co at CANDAS - Railway Construction under 277 Rly Co. R.E.	

Commanding 19th North'd Fus. (Railway Pioneers)

Army Form C. 2118

WAR DIARY
or
INTELLIGENCE SUMMARY

17th Bn Northumberland Fus (Railway Pioneers)

SHEET No 25

(Erase heading not required.)

15.(1)

Place	Date	Hour	Summary of Events and Information	Remarks and references to Appendices
ISBERQUES	1.2.17		A. Coy. at CANDAS. Railway construction under 249 & Rly Co. R.E.	
			B. Coy. at La Lacque. LA LACQUE. } Employed on construction of high	
			C. Coy. at Houleron HOULERON. } Railway Repair Shops BERGUETTE.	
			D. Coy. at LA ROUPIE.	
	16.2.17		A. Coy. moved to new billeting area at HOULERON.	
			Lieut Percy Smith resigned commission 24.1.17. London Gazette 24.1.17.	

[signature]
Lieut-Colonel,
Commanding 17th North'ld Fus (Railway Pioneers)

Vol 4

Army Form C. 2118

Sheet No. 26

17th Bn Northumberland Fus (Railway Pioneers)

WAR DIARY
or
INTELLIGENCE SUMMARY

(Erase heading not required.)

Place	Date	Hour	Summary of Events and Information	Remarks and references to Appendices
ISBERGUES	1.3.17 to 31.3.17		A & C Coys billeted at HOULERON — Employed on construction of Central Light Railway Workshops. B Coy billeted at LA LACQUE. D Coy billeted at LA ROUPIE.	Herdl Herdl
	30.3.17		Capt. & Adjt. G.W. Martin rejoined from temporary duty with the D.G.T., G.H.Q.	

G.W. Marden Capt.
for Lieut Colonel.
Commanding 17th Northumberland Fus.
(Railway Pioneers)

WAR DIARY
INTELLIGENCE SUMMARY
(Erase heading not required.) 17th Bn NORTHUMBERLAND FUS. (RAILWAY PIONEERS)

Army Form C. 2118
Sheet No. 27.

Place	Date	Hour	Summary of Events and Information	Remarks and references to Appendices
ISBERGUES	1.4.17		A & C Cos billeted in HOULERON B Co. billeted in LA LACQUE — Employed on Construction of Light Railway Repair Shops. D Co. billeted in LA ROUPIE	Cecil
	3.4.17		A, B, C and D Companies moved by train to POPERINGHE.	Cecil
	4.4.17		H.Q. Co. and Transport moved by road to POPERINGHE.	Cecil
	5.4.17		2nd Lieut N. Young proceeded to General Headquarters for duty with 25th A.T.Co. R.E. Lieut G.S.S. Gordon rejoined from duty with 25th A.T.Co. R.E.	Cecil
POPERINGHE	6.4.17		Battalion employed on formation & Construction of GREAT MIDLAND Railway, under R.C.E. II	Cecil
	8.4.17		A and B Companies moved to 'P' Camp C Company moved to Camp at A.30.b.4.2 (SHEET BELGIUM 28NW) D Company moved to TROIS TOURS CHATEAU	Cecil
	9.4.17		Bn. HQ moved to P Camp.	Cecil
	19.4.17		2nd Lieut R.G. Marple rejoined Battn. from attachment to Royal Flying Corps	Cecil
	21.4.17		2 Platoons B.C. moved to Camp at A.30.b.4.2 (Sheet BELGIUM 28NW)	Cecil
	26.4.17		3 or D Co. wounded. 1 wounded at duty	Cecil
	28.4.17		One Platoon 'B' Co. moved to Camp at A.30.b.4.2.	Cecil
	1.4.17 to 30.4.17		——— Ditto ———	Cecil
			BATTALION EMPLOYED ON CONSTRUCTION OF GREAT MIDLAND RAILWAY.	Cecil

Gwilbaclui Capt r/any
Comdg 17th Bn Northld Fus (Railway Pioneers)
for Lieut Colonel

Operation Order by Lieut: Col: W.D.V.O.King

Commanding 17th Bn. Northumberland Fusiliers (Railway Pioneers)

April 1st. 1917

No. 1.

1. Move	The Battalion will be held in readiness to move to-morrow the 2nd April 1917, time and place will be notified later.
2. Baggage	Officers Commanding Companies will arrange for all baggage, tools, and Company stores to be ready for loading at short notice.
3. Transport	One G.S. wagon and one G.S. limber will be detailed to each Company at 8/0am. for the purpose of carrying tools to destinations as required, in accordance with instructions issued - and ultimate loading of Company tools ready to entrain.
4. Blankets	Blankets will be stacked and labelled at 10-0am. at Company Headquarters. These will be collected and carted to the station at an hour to be notified later.
5. Working party	"A" Company will detail one Officer and 30 men to report at Battalion Orderly Room at 8/0am. for instructions. This party will include two joiners, with tools.
6. Water Tanks.	Company water tanks will be loaded on Company Tool wagons.
7. Latrine Buckets	Latrine buckets will be handed in to Tool store by Noon. Latrines will be left standing and clean.
8. Cookers	Dinners will probably be served in billets. Cookers will be ready for moving immediately after dinner time.
9. Maltese Cart	Maltese Cart will be at Medical Inspection Room at 8/0am. to be loaded and the mules returned to Transport Lines.
10. Passes	Company Commanders are authorised to sign any passes to proceed beyond Billeting area until 12-noon, for the purpose of collecting washing etc.,

(signed) G. W. Martin, Captain and Adjutant,

17th Battn: Northumberland Fusiliers (Railway Pioneers)

Issued at 11/45pm. April 1st. 1917

Operation Orders by Lieut:Col:W.D.V.O.King

Commanding 17th Bn. Northumberland Fusiliers (Railway Pioneers)

April 2nd 1917

---

1. Move — The verbal arrangements made for movement of motor lorries this evening will stand, except that Officers will report at the Headquarters' Mess at 7/0am. instead of 8/0am. Also the Officers' Mess Cart will collect the A and C Officers' kits.

2. Companies — "A","B","C","D" Companies, less the above party, and a rear party to be detailed by 'A','B','C', and 'D' Companies 1 Officer, 1 n.c.o. and 10 men per Company, who will remain behind for the night, will parade in sufficient time on the 3rd. instant as to arrive at BERGUETTE Station at 5/45am.

      DRESS - MARCHING ORDER.

3. Rear party — The personnel of rear party who remain behind will clean up billets and collect spare stores, and move by eight motor lorries on the 4th. instant, with any stores etc., left behind by the Battalion.

4. Blankets — Blankets of "A","B","C", and "D" Companies will be collected at 4/45 am.

5. Rations - Rear Party — Rations will be issued by the Quartermaster at Ration Store at 7/0am.

6. Transport — All transport will be moved under orders of the Quartermaster, later.

7. Kettles - Cooking — Officer Commanding Companies will arrange for all kettles to be removed from Cookers and picked up with Company blankets.

8. Telephones — Sergeant Key, with linemen, will arrange to dismantle wires and collect telephone instruments after 8/0am.

9. Officers' kits. — Officers' kits and rations for consumption on Wednesday will be loaded on motor lorry. Motor lorries will collect Officers' kits commencing at 6/0am. in the following order :-

    "D", "B", "A", "C" and "HQ"

(signed) G. W. Martin, Captain and Adjutant,

17th Bn. Northumberland Fusiliers (Railway Pioneers)

Issued at 2/15am. 3-4-1917

Operation Orders by Lieut: Col: W.D.V.C.King

Commanding 17th Bn. Northumberland Fusiliers (Railway Pioneers)

April 7th. 1917

---

1. Move   "C" Company will parade in Marching Order as directed verbally, at 8/0am. to-morrow, and will march to "D" Camp. map reference A.30.b.4.2., Company cooker and Transport as detailed will proceed with the Company.

    "A" and "B" Companies will parade in Marching order and March off at 2/0pm. to "P" Camp. Arrangements as directed verbally.

    "D" Company will parade in Marching order and march off at 6/0pm. to TROIS TOURS CHATEAU. Cooker will accompany, also two G.S. wagons will be placed at the disposal of the Company as arranged verbally.

(signed)   G. W. Martin, Captain and Adjutant

17th Bn. Northumberland Fusiliers (Railway Pioneers)

Issued at 10/15pm. 7-4-1917

Army Form C. 2118

WAR DIARY
or
INTELLIGENCE SUMMARY

(Erase heading not required.)

17TH Bn NORTHUMBERLAND FUSILIERS
(RAILWAY PIONEERS)

SHEET No 28

Instructions regarding War Diaries and Intelligence Summaries are contained in F. S. Regs., Part II. and the Staff Manual respectively. Title Pages will be prepared in manuscript.

Place	Date	Hour	Summary of Events and Information	Remarks and references to Appendices
POPERINGHE	1/7/17		BATTALION EMPLOYED ON CONSTRUCTION OF GREAT MIDLAND RAILWAY	
—	10/7/17		2nd Lt J J D Blaiklock joined Batt for Duty	
—	15/7/17		Temp/Lt G V Douglas relinquishes rank of Act Captain 31.3.17	
—	23/7/17		2nd Lt Tellice and 2nd Lt J De Bock Briely proceeded to England having been accepted for Commissions in Indian Army Reserve of Offrs.	
—	31/7/17		Battalion still employed on Great Midland Railway	

C W Harden Capt & Adj
for O.C. 17th N.F.

Army Form C. 2118

WAR DIARY
or
INTELLIGENCE SUMMARY 17th (Batt. Northumberland Fus.)
(N E RAILWAY PIONEERS)

SHEET No 29

Place	Date	Hour	Summary of Events and Information	Remarks and references to Appendices
POPERINGHE	1/6/17		BATT. employed on construction of Great Midland Railway	G.S.M.
"	11/6/17		D. Company move from Trois Tours Chateau to "P"Camp A15.d 4.4.	G.S.M.
"	12/6/17		"A" Company commenced work on Section of Light Railway	G.S.M.
"	1/6/17		2nd Lt R.G. MARPLE proceeded to England for posting to Indian Army	G.S.M.
"	2/6/17		3rd Lt NEVILLE appointed Transport Officer to Bn from 6-4-17	G.S.M.
"	12/6/17		Location of Bn.:- "A"-"D" + H.Q. Coy "P"Camp A15.d 4.4 "B"+"C" Coy A 30 central	G.S.M.
"	14/6/17		"A" Coy moved from "P"Camp to H 27.B.2.7. Light Railway construction	G.S.M.
"	22/6/17		A. Co. moved from H.24.b.2.7 to A.20.b.4.1	G.S.M.
"	23/6/17		2nd Lieut Swinthwaite proceeded to join 18th Bn Northd Fus (Pioneers) on posting	G.S.M.
"	26/6/17		B. Co. moved from A.20.b.4.1 to S.23.d.b.3 (Sheet Belgium 20SW)	G.S.M.
"	29/6/17		C. Co. moved from A.30.b.4.1 to S.28.B.5.0 (Sheet Belgium 20SW)	G.S.M.
"	30/6/17		Battalion employed on construction of Light Railways under A.D.L.R.(Y) Casualties during month - A. Co. 1 Killed 11 Wounded, B. Co. 2 Killed 6 Wounded, C. Co. 1 wounded, D. Co. 2 wounded.	G.S.M.

Guybashii Capt
for. Lieut Col.
Comdg Nth Northd Fusiliers

CONFIDENTIAL.   4

Officer i/c,
   Regular Infantry Section No.3.,
      GHQ. 3rd Echelon.

   Herewith please find War Diary of this Unit for the month of JULY 1917.

   Kindly acknowledge receipt.

                                             [signature]
                                                  Captain & Adjutant,
                              17th Bn. Northumberland Fusiliers (Railway Pioneers)

August 2nd 1917.

WAR DIARY or INTELLIGENCE SUMMARY

Army Form C. 2118

(17TH BN NORTHUMBERLAND FUS (RAILWAY PIONEERS))

SHEET No 20

Place	Date	Hour	Summary of Events and Information	Remarks and references to Appendices
POPERINGHE	1·VII·1917	–	HQ Coy D. Coy in Camp at "P" Camp (SHEET BELGIUM 28 – H.W. A.15.d.u.u.) A Company under Canvas at A.20.b.u.u. B Company under Canvas at S.22.d.6.3. (SHEET BELGIUM 20.S.W.) S.23.6.6.2) C Company under Canvas at S.29.b.2.0.	{ Battalion employed on Light Railway Construction under the A.D.L.R. Fifth Army } Ge.V. Ge.V.
	3·VII·1917	–	32110 Pte. McMillyorn A.Coy Accidentally Killed at A.28.b.8.9.	Ge.V.
	5·VII·17		17/386. Sgt. N. Welch 2 Brew A.Coy, 1 man 'C'.Coy, 1 man 'D'.Coy, 1 HQ.Coy, wounded A.15.d.u.u. also No.A.205440 Pte.10. Real A.S.C. M.T. wounded Kemmel & died same date	Ge.V.
	13·VII·17		Part 'A' Coy moved from A.30.b.4.1. to X.29.B.0.4.	Ge.V.
	19·VII·17		A Company moved from A.30.b.4.1. and X.29.B.0.4. to Training Camp E.17.b.7.1.	Ge.V.
	– ,, –		D Company 150 men and LIEUT DOUGLAS moved from A.15.d.4.4. to E.17.b.7.1.	Ge.V.
	– ,, –		B Company 2 Officers and 116 O.R. moved from S.23.d.6.3. to A.30.b.4.1.	Ge.V.
	28·VII·17		B Company Remainder of Coy moved from S.23.d.6.3. to A.30.b.4.1.	Ge.V.
	24·VII·17		'C' Company moved from S.28.b.3.0. to 'P' Camp A.15.d.u.u.	Ge.V.
	– ,, –		'A' Company moved from E.17.b.7.1. to 'P' Camp A.15.d.u.u.	Ge.V.
	26·VII·17		'C' – ,, – moved from 'P' Camp A.15.d.u.u. to E.17.b.7.1.	Ge.V.
	27·VII·17		'C' – ,, – moved from E.17.b.7.1. to P. Camp A.15.d.u.u.	Ge.V.
			'B' – ,, – moved from 'D' Camp to Canadian Camp	
	30·VII·17		The following units attached to Battalion for Railway Construction 18th NF(PIONEERS) – A.Coy / 18th Royal Scots (Pioneers) – (A.Coy 6th East York (PIONEERS) 'B' Company. 13th Glosters (PIONEERS) 'B' Company 5th Royal Sussex (PIONEERS) "A"&"D" Coys. 17th N.F. East York. Royal Scots and 1st Shift 18th NF moved out to positions made Routine order No.1 of 25·7·17 Commencing at 6pm. ‡Capt (Act. Major) E. Stamp Taylor awarded Military Cross by C in C	Ge.V. Ge.V. Ge.V. E. Stamp Taylor Capt. ‡ ao.o.c 17th NF

WAR DIARY
INTELLIGENCE SUMMARY

Army Form C. 2118.

Vol 2. 17th (S) Batt. Northumberland Fusiliers (Railway Pioneers).

SHEET No. 31

Place	Date	Hour	Summary of Events and Information	Remarks and references to Appendices
Peasslock	1/7		Companies employed on Railway Construction with 16th Corps Light Railway Advance. Coys located in Shifts No 1 Shift B 30.a. No 2 Shift B 23.c. Advanced H.Q. Formed Dump B 22.d. H.Q. still at P. Camp A 15 d 44. The following Units attached for Labour &c. 18th N.F. Pioneers. - A Coy 18 Royal Scots Pioneers. - B. Coy 13th Glouc. Pioneers B. Coy 5th Royal Sussex Pioneers - 172nd Labour & 148th Labour Corps.	Gen'l
	3/7		Shift moved up to camp in vicinity of C 26 A.	Gen'l
	5/7		1st Shift moved from C 26 A to P. Camp. 2nd Shift from C 26 A to B 30.a.	Gen'l
	6/7		2nd Shift moved to A 30 & 7.1. Ten rest	Gen'l
	7/7		1st Shift moved from P. Camp to C. 26 A.	Gen'l
	8/7		Lt J.O. Riddell proceeded Boat for duty from 31st to 3. D.	Gen'l
	9/7		2nd Shift moved from A 30 & 7.1. and P. Camp to B 30 29. B.	Gen'l
	15/7		Lt J.O. Riddell proceeded to join School of Military Engineering Chatham	Gen'l
			Battalion withdrawn from Light Railway Construction and located in P. Camp	Gen'l
	31/7		Casualties during month. Killed 3. Wounded 19. Wounded severely at duty 9.	Gen'l

Gallagher Capt. & Ag.
for O.C. 17th N.F. (Railway Pio)

Army Form C. 2118.

WAR DIARY
or
INTELLIGENCE SUMMARY 17TH (S) BATT. NORTHUMBERLAND FRS
(NE RAILWAY PIONEERS)

SHEET No 35 *(Erase heading not required.)*

Vol 25

Place	Date	Hour	Summary of Events and Information	Remarks and references to Appendices
ST JEAN	1/12/17		Battalion working under A.D.L.R II ARMY (NORTH) on Railway Construction Light Railway STEENBECK. ST JULIEN- LANGMARCK	Civil
"	10/12/17		2/Lieut W. Dinning joined Battalion for duty from 31st IBD	Civil
"	13/12/17		Lieut R. de P Dallin struck off strength from 27-11-17 England sick	Civil
"	17/12/17		3Lt R.E. transferred from Batt to R.E. Base Depot Rouen	Civil
"	18/12/17		Lt & Qr A. T. Tindill admitted to Hospital	Civil
"	19/12/17		Capt R.M. Lakeman rejoined Batt from course of instruction	Civil
"	21/12/17		2ND Lt F.W Smith rejoined Batt for duty from Hospital	Civil
"	27/12/17		Lieut W.D. Roberson transferred to R.E. Coy Stockton 20-11-17 1 Officer (Capt Lakeman) 1 O.R. wounds 2 O.R. slightly at duty during Dec?	Civil

G W Alderson Capt
A/Lt for O.C.
17th N.F.

WAR DIARY
or
INTELLIGENCE SUMMARY 17th (S) Batt. NORTHUMBERLAND FUSRs
(NE RAILWAY PIONEERS)

SHEET No 36

Vol 26

Place	Date	Hour	Summary of Events and Information	Remarks and references to Appendices
ST JEAN	1/7/18		Headquarters moved to BELG SHEET 28 A 23. C 2.3. Companies located c. 20 central	Circut Genl Recd Circul
	3/7/18		Capt R.W. Latham repard from Hospl (wounded) 2nd Lieut C.R.Marshall & 10 O.Runners to England for R.F.C.	Genl
	18/7/18		Companies moved as under:-	
			A. Coy 2 platoons 7H.CRT.JnO. A22. B. S. 7.	
			A. Coy 2 platoon Registry	
			B. Coy 2 platoons NUNEATON B 23 B 2 7.	
			B. Coy 2 platoons AGADIR B 30 C 5 8.	
			C. Coy 4 platoons C 20 A 5 3	
			D. Coy 4 platoons C 20 A 5 3.	
			Headquarters A 23. C. 2. 3.	
	31/7/18		Casualties during Month 10 R.Killed 1 O.R. wounded 4 O.R. wounded slightly at duty	

Geo Gardin Capt
A/g 17 NF for OC

26 (1)

Army Form C. 2118.

WAR DIARY
or
INTELLIGENCE SUMMARY 17th (S) Batt. NORTHUMBERLAND FUS
(NE RAILWAY PIONEERS)
SHEET No 37. *(Erase heading not required.)*

Vol 27

Place	Date	Hour	Summary of Events and Information	Remarks and references to Appendices
BELG SHT 28 NW A 23.C 2.3	1/2/18		Battalion employed on maintenance of Light Railway's and Tramways. NORTHERN SYSTEM.	Gully
	4/2/18		2ND Lieut N.WATSON slightly wounded at duty.	Gully
	28/2/18		Companies located as under from 28/2/18. A Company :- At ST.JEAN-BYFLEET. B. Company :- Canadian H.Q. Camp. & 109 Ry Coy R.E. Old Camp. C Company :- Nunecatow and Toronto. D Company :- BYFLEET. & AGADIR also RUGBY.	Gully
			Casualties during month	Gully
	10/2/18		17/608. Pte W.S.Blackburn accidentally killed	
	4/2/18		2nd Lt. N.Watson above slightly wounded at duty.	
	10/2/18		17/713. Pte T.Richardson accidentally wounded	

Guyjardine Capt for
OC. 17th Northd Fus (S)

Deputy Adjutant General,
G.H.Q. 3rd Echelon,
BASE.

    Herewith War Diary in respect of this Unit for the month of MARCH 1918, please.

                                  Captain &
                                  Adjutant,
    17th North'd Fusiliers (N.E.Rly Pioneers)

April 1st 1918.

Army Form C. 2118.

WAR DIARY
or
INTELLIGENCE SUMMARY 17th (S) Batt NORTHUMBERLAND FUSRS
(RAILWAY PIONEERS)

SHEET No. 38. *(Erase heading not required.)*

Place	Date	Hour	Summary of Events and Information	Remarks and references to Appendices
BELGIUM SHEET 28 N.W.	1/3/18		Head Quarters. A.23.C.2.3.	9/1 28
			A Company.	
			B. Company. BYFLEET C20.a.5.3 RUGBY C1.a.5.8.	
			Old CANADIAN H.Q CAMP. A22.B.5.7 109 Coy RE Camp. B7.a.7.6.	
			C. Company NUNEATON B23.7.2.8 TORONTO B1b.c.9.u	
			D. Company. BYFLEET C20.a.5.3 AGADIR. B30.d.1.5.	
	28/3/18		17/661 Cpl. F. Banks 'B'Coy. Awarded Meritorious Serv. Medal by Corps Commander for gallant conduct in assisting to save life from drowning	
			One O.R. wounded since died	
			Four O.R. wounded	
			Eight O.R wounded slightly (at duty)	

G.W. Harden Capt.
O/c 17th N.F. for O.C.

28/5

WAR DIARY

INTELLIGENCE SUMMARY

17th (S) Batt. Northumberland Fusiliers
(RAILWAY PIONEERS)

SHEET No. 39.

Army Form C. 2118.

Vol 2 of

Place	Date	Hour	Summary of Events and Information	Remarks and references to appendices
BELGIUM	1/4/18		SHEET 28 N.W.	
			Head Quarters A.23.c.2.3.	
			A Company BYFLEET. C.20.a.5.3. AGADIR. B.30.d.15.	Genl
			B Company BYFLEET. C.20.a.5.3. RUGBY C.1.a.5.8.	Genl
			C Coy CANADIAN CAMP. A.22.b.57. - 109 R.E. Coy Camp. B.7.a.7.6.	Genl
			D Coy NUNEATON. B.23.b.26. TORONTO. B.10.C.9.4.	Genl
FRANCE	13.4.18		SHEET 36 N.E. SHEET 27 S.E.	
			Batt. moved by rail from POPERINGHE to STEENBECK arrived 12.50AM 14-4-18.	
	14.4.18		moved to LE GRAND HASARD. Bivouac'd D.8.C.9.2. (A Coy E.13.C.1.8) (B Coy E.13.C.0.2) (C Coy D.18.a.2.4)	
			(D Coy D.17.D.1.2) (H.Q D.18.A.2.4)	
			Battalion attached to 15th Corps 1st AUSTRALIAN DIVISION. Preparing	
			defence positions.	
	21.4.18		moved into 1ST AUS. DIV. to new sector preparing defences W.9.3.8.8.	Genl
			W.10 D.0.3. W.20.C.3.6. to RAILWAY LINE. E.3. Batt. H.Q. V.24.a.2.5.	
	30.4.18		Same area. Preparing defence positions.	Genl
			Casualties during month: 1 O.R Killed - 20 O.R. wounded	
			(5 O.R. since died of wounds) 5 O.R. wounded at duty.	

Lew Barthim Capt Acting
For O.C. 17th N.F.

29

WAR DIARY or INTELLIGENCE SUMMARY

Army Form C. 2118.

17th (S). Batt NORTHUMBERLAND. FUSR. (NE RAILWAY. PIONEERS)

SHEET No 40.

Place	Date	Hour	Summary of Events and Information	Remarks and references to Appendices
FRANCE. SHEET 27 S.E.	1-5-18		Batt. attached to XV Corps - 1st Australian division preparing defences. H.Q. at V.24.A.25.	Genrl
	10-5-18		Batt. attached CRE. XV Corps Troops. Move to D.I.C.q.1. (Sheet 36A) preparing defences in neighbourhood of HAZEBROUCK.	G854
	29-5-18		Batt. transferred from 2nd Army to 1st Army XVIII Corps as temporary attachment to 52nd Division as Pioneer Batt. (by march route) (via AIRE 29th; DIVION 30th; CAMBLAIN L'ABBÉ 31st)	G854
	31-5-18		Batt. (less A Company) to VILLERS AUX BOIS W30.b.9.7 Sheet 36.B.S.E) Marched to billet at NEUVILLE ST VAAST.	G854
			Casualties - Capt. L.V. Gatt, RAMC + 2/Lt. J. Potts - Wounded in Action. 1. O.R. Killed 2. O.R. Wounded in Action 7. O.R. " " (at Duty)	G854

GSS Grohm Capt + Adjt
17th Novh Fus
A.O.C.

GSS Grohm Capt + Adjt
17th Novh Fus

ON HIS MAJESTY'S SERVICE.

CONFIDENTIAL.

WAR DIARY

of

17th Bn. Northd Fusiliers (N.E.Railway Pioneers)

M A Y 1918.

=*=*=*=*=*=*=*=

www.ingramcontent.com/pod-product-compliance
Lightning Source LLC
Chambersburg PA
CBHW081438160426

43193CB00013B/2318